Contemporary Family Policy

A comparative review of Ireland, France, Germany, Sweden and the U.K.

Mary Daly and Sara Clavero
School of Sociology and Social Policy
Queen's University
Belfast

IPA
INSTITUTE OF PUBLIC
ADMINISTRATION

THE DEPARTMENT OF SOCIAL
AND FAMILY AFFAIRS

First published in 2002
by the Institute of Public Administration
57-61 Lansdowne Road
Dublin 4
Ireland
for
The Department of Social and Family Affairs

www.ipa.ie

British Library Cataloguing in Publication Data
A catalogue record for this book is available from the British Library

ISBN 1 902448 79 0

Cover design by M and J Graphics Ltd., Dublin
Typeset by DTP Workshop
Printed by Staybro Printing Limited, Dublin

CONTENTS

List of Tables

List of Figures

Acknowledgement

This research was funded by the Families Research Programme of the Department of Social and Family Affairs. The support of the staff of the Family Affairs Unit of the department is gratefully acknowledged.

Foreword

The family is the most important unit in Irish society. Our families have shaped us all and it is increasingly recognised that families have a vital role to play in ensuring the development and well being of both individuals and of society as a whole.

But the family as we knew it in the past is facing new challenges. Many of these challenges are identified in this research study – including issues such as the change in the traditional family model and the increase in the numbers of mothers working outside the home.

This creates major pressures in terms of the caring needs of children, older people and people with disabilities who need care. And these pressures will increase in the coming decades as our population ages.

This government is committed to strengthening families by ensuring that families are at the centre of all our policies.

As minister with responsibility for family affairs, I want to make sure that public policy makes a real difference to families. That is why I am establishing the Family Support Agency which marks a further step forward in the development of effective and responsive services and supports for families today.

But if we want to strengthen and support families, we need to know much more about families and about family policy. That is why I am delighted to be able to commission and support research studies like this one. We need to know what works and what does not; what governments can and should do to support families and also what families are better able to do for themselves.

This study makes an important contribution to advancing our knowledge about what works in family policy in Europe. I would like to thank Professor Mary Daly and Ms Sara Clavero for their many hours of hard work in researching this project. And I can assure them that the lessons from this research will inform future policy development.

Mary Coughlan TD
Minister for Social and Family Affairs
August 2002

Executive Summary

Policy makers in Europe are having to radically rethink how the family is supported by public policy. In a climate where economic, social and demographic developments affect the family almost at every turn, policy makers have to work continuously to both update and transform policy.

Objectives and Scope of the Report

The subject matter of this report is the recent reform of family policy in Ireland and Europe. Funded by the Families Research Programme, its purpose is both to identify the most significant changes which have been made in Europe in the last ten years and to compare developments in Ireland with those in a selected number of other countries. In particular, Ireland is compared with France, Germany, Sweden and the United Kingdom (UK). The time period covered by the study is the 1990s, with all the information updated to the middle of 2001. Family policy for the purposes of the study is defined in a broad way. The report covers the following policy domains: cash payments for families with children, the support of lone parent families, family-related taxation, reconciling work and family life, childcare, care of the elderly, family support services and children's rights. As well as tracing and comparing the changes in policy, the report also examines some of the impacts associated with family policy. Matters such as the effects of policy on family poverty, the redistribution of income, fertility rates and the employment participation of mothers are each considered.

The implications of reform and the outstanding issues facing policy makers in Ireland are also discussed.

The report contains seven chapters as well as a brief introduction. The first chapter describes the historical development of family policy in Ireland, for the purpose especially of identifying the tradition and architecture of Irish social policy as it related to the family. The development of family policy in Europe is the subject matter of the second chapter, the goal being to identify similarities and differences in Ireland's approach to the family historically, in comparison with developments elsewhere. Having identified the general state of family-related policy in Ireland and elsewhere up until the late 1980s-early 1990s, the next two chapters go on to cover reform and change in the 1990s. Chapter 3 focuses on Irish reforms whereas Chapter 4 details the most significant developments in France, Germany, Sweden and the UK. Chapter 5 turns to impacts associated with family policy, considering some evidence on horizontal redistribution, poverty alleviation, fertility rates and employment levels among women. The next chapter draws out some policy issues facing Ireland, focusing on topics which have been the subject of debate and review as well as those which this research identifies as key issues facing Irish social policy. A brief overview chapter draws the report to a close.

Development and Focus of Policy on the Family in Ireland and Europe

Ireland's family policy developed very gradually. For a long time, it consisted mainly of child benefits, tax allowances for children and maternity benefits. In other words, the dominant concerns were how to assist families with the costs of children and also to provide income support to mothers who had recently given birth. An additional objective of Irish family policy historically was to support the family founded on marriage. The two main architects of family policy were the state and the Catholic Church, with the influence of the latter waning from about the 1970s on.

The approach taken at the beginning was very selective, for example only larger families received child benefit when it was first introduced in 1944, but it has broadened out over the course of time. In the 1970s, family policy came to include programmes to support the families of unmarried mothers and deserted wives. As it developed over time, family policy in Ireland assumed a more universalist cast, orienting itself to supporting all families with children (regardless of family size and income). However, the selectivist strand in Irish social policy in general is deeply rooted and has not been displaced by an ethos of universalism. Among the more notable features of the approach taken to the family in Ireland historically was the fact that state assistance to families was primarily given in the form of cash support rather than services. Services for families were quite under-developed in Ireland (as compared with some other European countries) and, where they existed, tended to be developed and run by the religious and voluntary sectors (though usually with substantial state funding). Looked at as a whole, one could say that Irish family policy provided rather limited assistance to families and that the guiding ethos was that families should take primary responsibility for their own welfare. Moreover, policy generally endorsed and supported a full-time homemaker role for women with the man as the sole provider for the family, i.e. it supported the male breadwinner family. The value of financial supports given to marriage (through the tax system) was greater than those for the support of families with children.

Looking across Europe, countries have varied considerably in the way that they have organised and developed their policy on the family. This diversity seems overwhelming but in fact there have been three main approaches taken by countries to the support of families with children. The first is a universal approach where all families, irrespective of the marital, financial and employment status of the parents, receive assistance from the state. This tends to be the approach taken in the Scandinavian countries. In the second model, support is tied to the father's employment, the cash benefit to the family is paid as a supplement to the father's wages. The continental European countries tended to follow this approach. The third approach, which generally characterises the English-speaking countries, not only differentiates between different types of families but directs the main support to families which are seen to be financially and morally deserving. Ireland does not fit easily into any of these approaches although its selective approach, especially at the outset, meant that it was closest to the English-speaking countries. However, the level of support provided in Ireland for families throughout most of the second half of the twentieth century was generally very low as compared with other countries. Nonetheless, Ireland's relative position improved significantly in the second half of the 1990s.

Reform of Family Policy in Ireland in the Last Decade

If Irish social policy historically was reluctant to consider the needs of the family as a concern of social policy in its own right, all that changed in the 1990s. That decade saw major developments in family policy in Ireland. A Commission on the Family was set up in 1996 to review existing provision and to make recommendations on how policy can help to strengthen families. A host of changes ensued following the publication of the Commission's report in 1998. Looking at the 1990s as a whole, the reforms made in family policy were of two major types.

The first trend was to consolidate existing family policy. The dominant change here was the very significant increases made to the value of child benefits. Between 1990 and 2001, for example, the value of child benefits rose by 327 per cent. Other developments included the increasing generosity and scope of benefits for carers of elderly and ill adults and the consolidation of several benefits for women rearing children on their own into the One-Parent Family Payment. In relation to lone parents and carers of elderly people, one could characterise reforms in the 1990s as recognising them as a sector of the population with legitimate welfare needs.

The second line of development in Irish family policy during the last decade was more 'transformative' in nature. This refers to a whole range of measures designed to reconcile work and family life and to raise the level of support to carers. Childcare was high on the policy agenda, with a lot of investment directed in particular to increasing the supply of childcare places. Making policy for the demand side has proved much more problematic, not least because this raises issues around the employment of mothers which has for long been contentious in Ireland. Along with the objective of raising the level of income support given to families with children, a further clear tendency of Irish policy in the last decade has been to prioritise children. Policy is heading in the direction of granting children some rights as citizens. This is radical in an Irish context, for the social rights of adults in Ireland have seldom been framed in a discourse of citizenship.

The development of services to support families is a third novel feature of Irish family policy over these years. In fact, this has been one of the main responses to the recommendations made by the Commission on the Family. Two types of family services are being developed. The first focuses on families in need, especially those living in disadvantaged areas. The second set of services focuses on providing counselling for couples experiencing difficulties and family mediation in cases of marital breakdown.

Reform of Family Policy in Europe in the Last Decade

While there is considerable variation in reforms being introduced in France, Germany, Sweden and the UK, it is possible to identify a number of common trends. The most widespread of these is what can be termed a move towards a welfare mix, whereby it is a policy goal to diversify the provision of services. Diversification has mainly taken the form of an increased role for the private sector in those countries which have traditionally adhered to a public service model. A second widespread emphasis in policy in European countries is the reconciliation of work and family life. This has had two expressions in policy. On the one hand, employed parents are given increased incentives and support to take time off work to care for their children. Both parents can be targeted in this regard but there is increased interest in encouraging fathers to take time off work to care for their young children. This type of reconciliation policy is by and large EU-driven. On the other hand, in the second type of reconciliation policy, there is a general move towards activating people to be employed. This could be said to have a certain reconciliation character in that male and female parents are increasingly encouraged to be economically active.

A move towards children's rights is a third identifiable trend in the policy landscape of the countries studied. This is also a two-fold initiative, involving both improved access for children to services which are oriented to their social rights (e.g. pre-school and other educational services as well as health services) and the introduction of political rights for children (with a special emphasis on their right to participate in decisions which directly affect them).

A fourth identifiable European trend is towards a closer focusing of family support on parenthood and parenting (as against marriage). Parental responsibilities are more emphasised today, with the financial obligations of fathers being especially reinforced. There is also a move away from a tax privileging of marriage and a tendency to grant non-married couples similar rights and responsibilities to married couples.

A fifth tendency is to support families with the indirect or opportunity costs of children. This, for example, is to be seen in the moves to support families with the costs of childcare.

Developments in Ireland are similar in some regards but they are for the most part in a different direction. In regard to the first general European trend, the move to a welfare mix, it is not easy to place Ireland because historically services have been undeveloped and the voluntary sector has played a large role in service provision. There is a move to involve the private sector more in relation to both the provision of care for children and for the elderly. There is also a move to involve employers more in providing childcare. Ireland shares with other countries the trend towards the greater reconciliation of work and family life and has, for example, increased the length and generosity of maternity benefits and introduced (unpaid) parental leave and leave for carers. However, Ireland lags considerably in regard to paternity benefits and paid parental leave. In considerable contrast, Ireland is in the vanguard when it comes to children's rights, especially their political rights. The National Children's Strategy, which was launched in 2000, set out a broad-ranging framework of children's rights and services and the realisation of these is proceeding. The fourth trend in other countries – refocusing on the responsibilities of parents – is on the agenda in Ireland but has not advanced very far. For example, there have been no very strong moves to shift the support for lone parents and their children either to fathers or by compelling the parents to take up paid work. Ireland is also adrift of the trend to shift assistance to families from the direct costs of children to indirect costs. This type of move is expressed by prioritising payments for childcare over general cash supports to families (such as child benefits). Ireland has, as we have seen, chosen to prioritise child benefit as the conduit of support to the family whereas in other countries the costs associated with parents' employment are increasingly supported by the state.

Some Impacts Associated with Family Policy

Family policy is potentially very wide-ranging in its impact. Four areas of impact are especially relevant. These are: income redistribution, poverty, fertility rates and the employment rates of mothers. However, it is difficult to be specific about outcomes since causality is almost impossible to establish. Given this, it is more accurate to speak in terms of 'associated effects' and to conceive of the impact of family policy in a broad way.

In regard to its income redistributive effect (measured as the impact of an extra child on the disposable income of a family on average earnings), policy in Ireland, as in the UK, effects less redistribution to families with children than does policy in Sweden, France or Germany. This is likely to be due to the fact that, despite the recent increases in child benefits, Ireland still offers a lower level of support to families with children than either Sweden, France or Germany. For similar reasons, poverty among families with children is also high in Ireland and the UK.

With respect to behavioural effects associated with family policies, there is very little evidence to suggest that such policies affect family size. However, a number of research studies have shown a significant impact of the so-called 'reconciliation policies' (i.e. maternity leave, parental leave and childcare) on the labour force participation patterns of mothers. In general, this relationship has been shown to be positive. For example, maternity and parental leave provisions seem to strengthen women's attachment to the labour market by: (a) providing incentives to enter employment prior to childbirth, and (b) speeding up the return to work after childbirth. The effects of the availability of childcare services on the employment behaviour of mothers are less clear. However, it does appear that the greater availability of a range of childcare options increases the labour force participation rates of mothers.

Challenging Issues in Relation to the Family for Policy in Ireland

The family figured quite prominently in policy debate and review during the 1990s. In this debate four specific issues have dominated. The first is very general and concerns the articulation or elaboration of the principles of family policy in Ireland around three fundamental questions: (a) the functions of the family, (b) its place in society and (c) the nature of family relationships. The second issue concerns the move from a male breadwinner model of social provision to the individualisation of social rights and entitlements. Although this issue has been debated for very different reasons and in a variety of contexts, a concern underpinning much of the debate is that of horizontal equity (that is, equity across households with and without children). The question of how to develop a system of childcare provision that is neutral with respect to parents' choices in relation to employment participation and the care of their children is another issue that has been prominent in popular debate in Ireland over the past few years. A core principle arising out of this debate is that support should be equitable and so should be provided to parents regardless of their income and employment status.

Finally, debates on lone parenthood have centred around two issues, namely: (a) the extent to which public policy should encourage or compel lone parents to be employed, and (b) the extent to which it should encourage, rather than discourage, joint parenting.

Although these issues have been thoroughly examined in a number of both external and internal reviews undertaken in the last few years, the majority of these exercises failed to reach a consensus and hence they remain unresolved. One way of gaining a better insight into the nature of these issues is to place them in a wider international context.

The experience of other countries suggests a number of important lessons.

a   There is a need to take an integrated as well as a multidimensional approach with respect to care. This means taking account of the needs of the person providing care as well as those of the care receiver. In relation to the care of children, for example, policy must ensure that the needs of parents are balanced with those of children, just as in the case of care of the elderly and other adults the needs of the care giver and the person receiving care have to be both provided for.

b   There is a gender dimension in policies which attempt to reconcile work and family life; this needs to be recognised and addressed. Many reconciliation policies are framed in such a way as to encourage mothers to take parental leave. The gender imbalance that this causes and the way it might act to perpetuate gender inequality need to be countered by policy. In this regard, the situation of fathers and the role of policy in promoting active fatherhood need to receive a prominent place in policy making.

c   Equity considerations in relation to the family are complex, not least because both horizontal and vertical equity are involved. Both kinds of equity consideration need to be balanced in family and other policies. In addition, families require assistance with both the direct and indirect costs of children.

Introduction

Compared with pensions and health care, the family has
tended to be the poor relation in social policy. This situation
is changing as the family is drawn more and more into the
embrace of public policy. This report reviews family policy
in Ireland in an international perspective. One of its objectives
is to identify the policy approach taken to the family in Ireland
and other European countries and to show how family policy
has changed in the last decade or so. Throughout, the most
interesting set of questions centres upon how Ireland
compares with other countries, in terms of its programmes,
the objectives and values underlying family policy and the
general trajectory of policy development. The research was
designed in such a way as to include a set of countries which
exemplify quite different approaches to the family and indeed
social welfare in general. In fact the five countries studied
encompass more or less the range of variation in regard to
policy on the family that is to be found in Europe. Along with
Ireland, the study focused on France, Germany, Sweden and
the UK to see how they approached the family historically and
how they are adapting their family-related policies to
changing social and economic conditions.

Why Study Family Policy?

The analysis of policy on the family has much to commend it.
In actual fact the family is a useful way of accessing a
country's general policy model. For one thing, it cuts across
different policy domains and so leaves one unencumbered by

the usual boundaries between policies, which are often administrative in origin. Secondly, the family as a departure point facilitates a comprehensive analysis, in that all policies can be examined on such fundamental questions as whether they take the individual or the family as the unit of reference, whether for income compensation purposes they take account of family size, and so forth. A third reason as to why the family provides a good access route to understanding contemporary social policy is because it is a field of policy showing great innovation. Most countries have had to concern themselves more actively with the family in the last decade or so and there are interesting, and from a policy perspective exciting, developments to be uncovered.

There are many reasons why social policy has to be increasingly oriented towards the family. In the developed world today, the context of public policy making on the family is in the process of being transformed. Four main social changes are noteworthy in this respect. The first is the challenge to the traditional family model. The traditional family – of father as breadwinner and mother at home looking after house and children – is no longer the sovereign model of family in industrialised countries. In the USA for example, the so-called average family, comprising father, homemaker mother and two children, represents less than 5 per cent of the total (*International Social Security Review*, 1994, p. 4). Family forms are becoming more diversified. As well as the lone-parent family, the range of family types is expanding to include greater numbers of informal partnerships, one-person households and reconstituted families. Ireland too is in the throes of a trend towards greater family diversity (Fahey and Russell, 2001). One implication for policy is that it can no longer take one family form as its reference point but must envisage, and indeed plan for, a range of family types. An additional challenge is that policy making is taking place in a time of transition which means that policy has to respond to new needs (*International Social Security Review*, 1994, p. 4). Thirdly, the breakdown of the traditional family makes it even more difficult for a country to ensure the wellbeing of children because it means that not as much reliance can be placed as in the past on the family for this purpose.

A second trend is the growth in women's employment. This is a deeply-ingrained feature of changing societies; the fact that it is taking place more or less independently of the state of the economy and national employment rates suggests that it is a fundamental social shift. While it is a general trend almost everywhere (Daly, 2000), the scale and pace of the rise in female employment in Ireland over recent years is equivalent to something of a social revolution. For example, the proportion of Irish women working outside the home grew by a massive 60 per cent in the ten years between 1988 and 1998. Mothers are at the forefront of this trend. The main challenge to policy, in this scenario, is to increase the compatibility between gainful employment and family responsibilities. Hence, one sees a growing interest among policy makers in Europe, Ireland included, in provisions such as childcare, parental leave and other measures which blur the formerly stark boundaries between work and home. 'Reconciliation of work and family' has not just entered the social policy lexicon but it has become an active (and innovative) domain of policy.

The third challenge is the emergence of the dual-income family. Families are finding it necessary and desirable for both parents to be in employment. The reasons for this vary. In Ireland dearer housing costs and more expensive lifestyles and modes of consumption are among the main financial reasons. But social factors are also at work. Women's increased participation in employment is an expression of their growing wish for independence, as represented by a life outside as well as within the home. This poses two major challenges for policy. One implication of dual-earner families is that they alter and indeed accentuate the direct and indirect costs of children (*International Social Security Review,* 1994, p. 6). So, policy makers must not just compensate families financially for the cost associated with having children but make it attractive for people to have children. A second relevant challenge for social policy is to assist one-income families.

The changing situation affecting the growth in the size of the elderly population also poses a set of fundamental challenges to public policy in general and policy on the family in particular. While Ireland has yet to experience the bulge in the elderly population facing most European Union (EU) states, care of the elderly is becoming an increasingly important issue for policy makers here as elsewhere. The supply of care is decreasing – as more women of all ages are drawn into the workforce – at the same time as the demand for such care is growing. The demographic changes alluded to above also serve to significantly alter the policy context surrounding care for the elderly. Family breakdown and the growth of one-person households act in the long-term to reduce the private/family resources available for care. Hence, the state must take a more active role. In addition, changing norms around family solidarity and the obligations associated with family membership spell a greater responsibility for the statutory sector in care of the elderly.

This, then, is the general context within which policy making is taking place in Ireland and elsewhere. All countries vary in the extent to which they are affected by these developments. In the case of Ireland, the developments around care – of both children and the elderly – are among the most keenly-felt issues of the day. The movement of women in such large numbers into the labour force is occasioning a set of adjustments which are not only to be felt in individual families and communities, but have ramifications for the way in which people make sense of their own obligations and live out their lives in the context of what they understand to be public and private responsibilities.

What is Family Policy?

Some people think that family policy is an easy subject for analysis – it does, after all, refer to an area that is familiar to almost everyone. Often, however, the things we most take for granted can be the hardest to study objectively. This is the case with the family. It may not be obvious for example that the family needs to be defined and that there are quite a number of alternative ways of defining it (e.g. biological connections, the composition of the family unit, the presence of children, the nature of the relationship between members, and so forth). For this and other reasons there is no consensus about how family policy is best conceptualised and studied.

Family policy has tended to be conceived of in what appears today to be a narrow way (Sgritta, 1990). Usually family policy has been taken to refer to policies for families with children and, more specifically, to cash payments to assist families with the costs of child rearing (child benefits as they are now most popularly known). One of the earliest definitions of family policy was that used by Kamerman and Kahn (1978). They defined it as deliberate governmental actions taken towards the family. In other words, the family has to be the specific focus for policy to merit the epithet 'family policy'. This view is contested, mainly by those who argue that policy can affect the family without it ever being specifically targeted at the family.

This links into a wider debate about definitions centring on whether one should treat family policy as a field or perspective. In the former approach family policy consists of a demarcated field of policies with particular objectives (relating to the family in the first instance but not by any means limited to it). The relevant policy fields could include welfare policy, incomes policy, population policy, health policy, and so forth. The alternative view – family policy as perspective or criterion – is much broader and does not limit its ambit to particular fields but rather searches for the impact of all or most policies on the family. In one example of such an approach, the criterion 'family wellbeing' has been used to interrogate a range of policies (Zimmerman, 1992). The significance of all of this for the researcher is that one must be very clear from the outset about what one means by 'family policy'. In addition, when some of the existing literature on family policy is examined it is clear that it has taken a limited approach (in focusing mainly on cash benefits and tax allowances for families with children). A broader approach is adopted here.

Definitions and Terms in this Research

In this research the debate about what constitutes family policy is managed by viewing it as both field and perspective.

Hence attention is directed to the main instruments of family policy (cash payments, tax allowances, social services) as well as a number of fields in which policy is most likely to affect the family (social security, income, taxation and employment policy). It will be obvious therefore that the study does not use the traditional (narrow) definition of family policy as relating only to the support of families with children. This kind of definition fails to reflect the extent to which policy has itself moved on to extend its remit and effects beyond one narrow family arena or form.

This means that in examining policy one must ask general as well as specific questions. What constitutes a family for policy purposes? To what extent do different programmes vary in how they regard and treat families and their individual members? How are relations and responsibilities among family members viewed and treated? Where and when does family responsibility end? What kind of division of labour as regards the welfare of family members is envisaged between the family and the state? These and other questions may be so taken for granted that they are rarely explicitly asked. It may not be obvious, for example, that the category of lone parent is used, and makes sense, only when the two-parent family is taken as the point of reference. Nor indeed do people find it remarkable that social policies 'imagine' and make assumptions about what happens within families, even if they do not always intervene in families. The point to be emphasised is that the extent to which policies differentiate between married and unmarried people, the assumptions they make about whether benefits should be earned or not and about whether parents should maintain their children, are all the result of decisions. What follows from this analytically is that one must be conscious of the norms and assumptions that are built into policy. In addition, the perspective on the family may not be clearly defined anywhere and so has to be 'excavated' through an analysis of different programmes in terms of both the fine print of entitlement and the norms and assumptions which underlie them.

So as to bring conceptual order to the research, it is useful to think in terms of 'family-related policy packages'. This allows one to approach public policy in a more open way, moving beyond the narrow understanding of family policy as provision for families with children. The framework which guided the research is reproduced in the Appendix. This report includes as family policy the following:

- cash payments and tax allowances for the family as a unit;
- benefits for parents, spouses and children in different kinds of families;
- childcare programmes;
- provision for the care needs of elderly and ill adults;
- services for the support of families.

There are a few further points about our approach which merit emphasis.

First, it should be noted that provision for the elderly is included in the definition of family policy. This follows from the belief that care of the elderly is most often in Ireland (as it is elsewhere) a matter for the family and that social policy plays a key role in endorsing or changing that pattern. Second, while the focus in different parts of the research is on the specific areas of provision as listed, a country's mix of provisions is also of central interest. It is possible to identify an overall approach to the family even in those countries which do not have an explicit, clearly demarcated family policy. Thirdly, this broad package approach has been chosen in recognition of the fact that social policies are much more than just a series of measures to help people when they need it – they reach deep into the fabric of society. They neither emerge spontaneously nor function independently of broader social norms. It follows that the policy approach taken in relation to the family in a country, if it is so deeply embedded, affects not just individual behaviour but the very structure of the society itself. It may be either cause or consequence of social stability or change. Against this kind of backdrop, it is important to keep the micro or individual perspective in mind as well as the more macro or societal view.

The Approach Taken to Comparison

This research also has the added methodological challenge of studying family policy in a comparative context. What matters most for comparative research is that the concepts and design of the study are broad enough to include and accommodate developments across countries (rather than biased towards one country's experience). This is especially important when the focus of research is family policy because, as we shall see, there are different types of family policy in place across Europe.

A first principle of the methodological approach adopted in this research, then, is to allow for variation. In practice this means that the country cases have been selected so as to, on the one hand, maximise variation and, on the other, control for it. A second principle is that context matters. An expansion or residualisation of a benefit or service can mean something very different in a welfare state founded on the principle of universalism compared with one oriented to minimum or basic provision. Third, the report adopts a case study methodology – analysing provision in its contextual setting. While it may not always be reported as such in the text, the analysis has proceeded by first looking at provision in each country in detail and, only when this was done, undertaking a comparison across countries. This kind of context-rich methodology has no real competitor when it comes to the study of change. Its strengths lie in its capacity to take account of the complexity of national policies as well as in enabling limited generalisations to be made across countries. A fourth principle of the approach adopted here is that it starts with a series of open questions about change. Searching for convergence or divergence, because it is such a specific starting point, forecloses too many options. Rather, what matters for the purpose of this research is how countries cope with the challenges which changing economic and social patterns throw up and whether their responses are for them traditional or innovative.

The Structure of the Report

Family policy as it developed in Ireland up to the early 1990s is the theme of the first chapter of the report. This describes the architecture and history of Irish social policy as it related to the family. The main details of relevant programmes, policy instruments and the overall objectives of policy up to around 1990 are described. The approach taken in Ireland is interesting in its own right but also because it is only one approach from a range of measures. The next chapter looks therefore at family policy across countries, in order to identify other types of family policy and indeed the different approaches to family policy as they developed historically in Europe. Having identified the general state of family-related policy in Ireland and elsewhere up until the late 1980s-early 1990s, the next part of the report goes on to deal with reform and change. The 1990s and the period up to July 2001 are the focal point in this regard. The procedure here again is to detail Irish developments in one chapter before going on to compare these with developments in France, Germany, Sweden and the UK. These two chapters – 3 and 4 – are the centrepiece of the report. Chapter 5 considers the most up-to-date evidence on the impacts associated with family policy. The effects on horizontal redistribution, poverty alleviation, fertility rates and employment levels among women are each given space here. The next chapter draws out some policy issues facing Ireland, focusing on topics which have been the subject of debate and review as well as those which this research identifies as key issues facing Irish social policy. A final brief overview chapter draws the report to a close. A bibliography and an appendix accompany the text. The appendix describes the framework of analysis and the key questions used for the research.

It should be noted that all amounts are presented in euro. The exchange rate used for the conversion of sterling and for Sweden the Kronor (SEK) is that which prevailed on March 26, 2002.

Chapter 1

Family Policy in Ireland up to 1990

To identify the approach taken to the family, one must look not only at policy measures themselves but also at general values in relation to the family which are embodied in law and the Constitution.[1] The legal architecture of a country is to be seen as setting the general frame for social policy, establishing norms and values as much as prescribing on matters such as marriage, property relations and parenthood. In Ireland the family based on marriage has been the guiding model of all social policy. In this regard public policy took its cue from the Constitution[2] – hence social policy was primarily concerned with the protection and enhancement of the family founded on marriage. Historically this saw policy focus on the male breadwinner family, a desire to assist families with the costs of children and a concern about providing for widows. Constitutional priorities predetermined other aspects of family policy as well: the emphasis should be on the unit as a whole and, to the extent that people were applying for benefits in their own right, they should be treated on the basis of their family status rather than as individuals.

As the Interim Report of the Commission on the Family (1996, p. 13) pointed out, family policy in Ireland takes the form of a loose amalgam of different areas of policy. The most prominent set of family-related policies consists of the measures oriented to the financial support of families with children. These include not only cash assistance with the costs of children but also measures to support mothers rearing children on their own and parents in general. Support to families is given not only through the social welfare system but also by means of allowances and exemptions for tax purposes. To these one must add social services as another relevant domain of family policy. The provisions in each of these broad areas up to 1990 will first be described, followed by an analysis of them in terms of underlying objectives and their general orientation.

1.1 The Remit and Form of Family Policy in Ireland

Utilising the broad conception of family policy as discussed earlier, this section considers, along with measures oriented towards the support of children, more general income support measures and services as they affect the family.

1.1.1 Income Support to Families with Children

Historically there have been four pillars of income support to families with children in Ireland:

- cash payments to families with children (most widely known as child benefit);
- additional payments to families, with children, dependent on social welfare (known as child dependant allowances);
- cash payments to families with children where earnings are low (the Family Income Supplement);
- assistance through the tax system (child tax allowances or additions to tax exemption limits for tax payers on low income).

Each will be briefly discussed in turn.

Child benefit was and remains the cornerstone of social policy on the family in Ireland. The benefit was introduced on a general basis in 1944, similar allowances for civil servants having been put in place in 1926.[3] Targeted from the outset on large families – at the time of their introduction the benefit was paid only for third and subsequent children aged under sixteen years – children's allowances as they were then known were financed from general tax revenues. Given that the average family size at the time was two children, it is likely that the roots of children's allowances in Ireland lay mainly in a concern about the poverty risk and financial needs of large families (Farley, 1964, p. 71; Powell, 1992, pp. 213-4). The children's allowances were paid to the head of the household[4] (effectively fathers) until 1974 when mothers became the official beneficiaries. The allowances were extended in 1952 to families with two or more children (but paid at a lower rate) and in 1963 to families with one or more children (with payment rates varying according to the number of children in the family). In 1973 the qualifying age was raised to eighteen years for children in full-time education or training and for those who were disabled. In the context of the nature of Irish social policy at the time and subsequently, children's allowances had one distinguishing feature. While initially in line with the strong selectivist orientation of Irish social policy, the universalist thrust which they acquired from the 1960s onwards makes them a unique benefit in an income support system which had for so long tied benefits to employment status and need.

A second pillar of income support is the child dependant allowances which have for long been a feature of Ireland's social welfare system. These payments to benefit recipients, intended to compensate them for income need associated with rearing a family, developed gradually in the Irish social welfare system. They were rationalised in 1952 when allowances became payable under most schemes for 'adult dependants' and up to two dependent children (Maguire, 1986, p. 262). Allowances for third and subsequent children were introduced in 1960. The recognition of family costs was however fairly selective, and the development of these allowances over time was quite ad hoc. Children dependent on old age pensioners were not provided specifically for until 1964, for example. At the time when the Commission on Social Welfare reported in 1986, there were thirty-six different child dependant allowances in operation.

Family Income Supplement is a payment made to workers who are rearing families on low earnings. It represents an alternative type of anti-poverty strategy to social welfare since it seeks to alleviate the unemployment trap by increasing the net gain from low-paid employment. One of its likely side-effects, though, is to act as a subsidy to low wages.

The Irish provision was closely modelled on a similar programme introduced in Britain in 1972. Ireland and Britain are, in fact, the only European countries to have such a designated in-work benefit for families. Introduced here in 1984, entitlement is calculated as 60 per cent of the difference between gross pay (since 1998 net pay) and a ceiling which is calculated on the basis of the number of children in the worker's family. In order to qualify people must be working for at least thirty-eight hours a fortnight. At the last count (2000) some 13,062 families were receiving the supplement (Department of Social, Community and Family Affairs, 2001). Low take-up tends to be endemic to this type of measure. Irish take-up rates are estimated to be in the region of 20 to 45 per cent (depending on the definition used) (Commission on the Family, 1998, p. 153).

Child tax allowances form the fourth pillar of financial support for families with children. These allowances for children have a long history in Ireland, in fact they existed since the foundation of the state. Once children's allowances were introduced in 1944, a simultaneous reduction in child tax allowances was made in order to offset the possibility of greater benefit to tax payers (as distinct from non-tax payers who at that stage formed the majority of the population). This change introduced even further selectivity to children's allowances. The effect of the measure, which was in existence until 1954, was to restrict the net gains from different improvements in children's allowances to families which were either below the threshold for income tax or not assessed for tax (Commission on Social Welfare, 1986, p. 36). The relative generosity of Irish child tax allowances varied considerably over time. In the 1920s the child tax allowances were equivalent to between a quarter and a fifth of the tax allowance for a single person; in the 1930s they rose to 40 per cent and then to 48 per cent and between 1956 and 1959 they peaked at 67 per cent (Kennedy, 1989, pp. 92-94). By 1986 they were equivalent to only 7 per cent of the tax allowance for a single person. They were actually abolished in that year, mainly on the grounds that they were inequitable. The coalition government in power at that time intended this to be part of a big shake-up in income support for families with children. However, although the children's allowance was renamed child benefit in that year, it was not significantly increased in value. In 1989 a modified form of child tax allowances was reintroduced in the form of a tax exemption of €254 for children in low-income families. Such a marginal approach prevails to the present day, although the exemption limits have been raised moderately over time.

1.1.2 *Other Income Support Measures for Families*

Apart from social policy measures directed specifically at families with children, Ireland offers families income protection by virtue of a number of benefit programmes for women in various family situations.

An inclination towards protecting the traditional family gave provision for widows a high priority in Irish social policy. They were among the first groups to be provided for, taken out of poor relief by the introduction of specific (social insurance and social assistance) provision for them in 1935. This, in the form of contributory and non-contributory widows pensions, gave expression to the state's willingness to take over the man's provider role upon his death. Widows pensions, in providing only for a spouse, are an implicit support for marriage. Over time the qualifying conditions for these benefits were altered, principally to eliminate a qualifying age threshold for widows without children and also to raise the age at which a 'child' can be considered as dependent to take account of rising educational standards and achievements.

From about the 1970s on, social policy in Ireland began to broaden its understanding of what constitutes a family to recognise other family types (e.g. lone mothers). Provision for deserted wives and lone mothers (or 'unmarried mothers' as they were then termed) was in the vanguard in this respect. In 1970 a means-tested deserted wife's allowance was introduced, modelled on the non-contributory allowance for widows. A social insurance version of this provision was introduced in 1973. In actual fact, both of these provisions were directed at mothers rather than wives, since only women with dependent children qualified. Following a recommendation by the Commission on the Status of Women (1972) that unmarried mothers who choose to keep their children should receive a social welfare payment, a social assistance allowance for unmarried mothers was introduced in 1973. Although the Commission envisaged a short-term payment, in actual fact the allowance could, subject to a means-test, be paid until the child was aged eighteen years (or twenty-one if in full-time education). These two provisions, while they represented a significant departure in terms of the state's recognition of not just the existence but the needs of women-headed families, also served to institutionalise a social assistance-oriented approach to deal with such families and to entrench a 'contingency' bent in Irish social policy (that is, by tying income support to the experience of a particular set of circumstances).

1.1.3 Treatment of Families in the Tax Code

Families have been recognised in the tax code in Ireland since the foundation of the state. Such recognition has taken two forms: tax allowances for children (discussed under section 1.1.1 above) and higher tax allowances for married couples as compared with single tax payers. The basic principles of income tax in Ireland are that: (a) each taxpayer pays according to his or her means on a common basis with everybody else in the same position, and (b) basic needs should be met before income becomes liable to tax. Hence the presence of dependants within a family unit (i.e. dependent spouses[5] and children) has been acknowledged.

Looking at the period up until 1990, the following were the most significant features of the taxation of families in Ireland:

• the recognition of lone parents as a distinctive category within the tax system with the introduction in 1979 of the One Parent Family Allowance: This consists of an additional tax relief[6] for parents who are widowed, deserted, separated, or unmarried and are raising dependent child(ren) on their own. In the year following its introduction, the amount of the additional allowance was doubled (from €317 to €635) and since then its value has been rising steadily, to equal the value of the allowance for a single person in the year 2000-01 (€5,968).

- the extension, in 1980, of the special personal allowances and rate bands for single-earner married couples to dual earner married couples: This measure was enacted in response to the Supreme Court decision on the case of *Murphy v. The Attorney General* in which a dual-earner couple challenged the compulsory aggregation of the salaries of spouses for tax purposes. As a result of that decision, all married couples, whether with one or two incomes, have benefited from double the personal allowance and rate bands applicable to single individuals.[7]

- the abolition of the child tax allowance in 1986, on the grounds of 'fairness' since it was worth more to higher income earners: From the time of its introduction in the early 1920s, the value of the child tax allowance with respect to that of the allowance for married couples was subject to wide variation. However, from 1968/69, the value of the allowance began to decline steadily until its abolition.

- the introduction of a tax for children in low-income families in 1989: From then until 1994, its value was gradually increased from €254 to €571 (first and second child) and €825 (third and subsequent child). These values have since remained unchanged.

1.1.4 Benefits for Working Parents

Historically maternity was the only concern of working parents recognised by Irish social policy.

As elsewhere, maternity benefits in Ireland consisted of a cash grant at the time of the birth and payments during maternity leave from employment. Such benefits date much further back than child or family allowances, having been introduced in Europe as early as 1883 (Gauthier, 1999, p. 949). Ireland varies from this general pattern, however. A social insurance based cash grant for maternity existed until 1983. This was originally introduced with social insurance in

1911 and was successively reformed so that by the 1930s and 1940s it reached some 40 per cent of all births (Cousins, 1995, p. 108).[8] A new means-tested version of the grant was introduced in 1953 but its history thereafter is one of gradual decline. Today its value is €10 and since it is paid only to mothers with a medical card it was in 1996 received by only 2,486 new mothers. No maternity pay existed in Ireland until 1953 when, nearly a decade after the children's allowances, a maternity allowance for insured women was introduced. This provided a flat-rate payment for twelve weeks, six weeks before and after the birth. Although it was intended for employed women, the conditions were such that it could be claimed by women who had not been in employment for some time but had kept their contributions updated by credits (Cousins, p. 108). While an earnings-related supplement was added to the allowance in 1973, there was little development in relevant provision until 1981 when a fully earnings-related benefit for women in employment at the time of confinement was introduced. This provided a statutory entitlement to maternity leave of fourteen weeks at a wage replacement level of 80 per cent for most employed women.[9] The wage replacement level was cut to 70 per cent in 1984 and the allowance was extended in 1991 to insured part-time workers earning over €32 a week (as part of a general move to improve the social rights of part-time workers).

Whether women not in employment should be entitled to the maternity payment has been a source of contention in Ireland at different points in time. Historically these women gained entitlement through their husband's social insurance. Following the 1981 reform, many non-employed women gained entitlement through their credited contributions. This entitlement was abolished in 1992, however, which means, as Cousins (1995, p. 110) points out, that the only specific maternity provision for women who are not in employment is the means-tested maternity grant together with the possibility of payments for expenses incurred through the discretionary supplementary welfare allowance scheme. A considerably smaller proportion of births – 30 per cent – are covered by maternity allowance as compared with fifty years ago.

1.1.5 Services for Families

This has been a very underdeveloped field in Ireland, the idea of 'family services' having little or no historical grounding. Childcare for example, up to recently anyway, was understood and used to refer to services for children at risk and the term was usually used to refer to the 'protective', often institutional, services provided for children by the state. These date as far back as the early nineteenth century and encompass voluntary provision by religious orders on the one hand and state-mandated provision on the other. Given that the latter was often also provided by the religious orders, there was for all intents and purposes little difference between the two. However it is important to note that reformatories and industrial schools were legislated for from the middle of the nineteenth century so as to provide for children in need of state control or 'protection'. This was provision for a very specific type of family need, however.

In general cash benefits rather than services have been the dominant response of Irish social policy to need. Apart from these, care (in the form of institutional provision) was the only other form of provision available. One of the main blocks to the development of services was the privileged position accorded and arrogated to itself by the Catholic Church. To the extent that services were needed – and ideally the Catholic Church's view was that families and communities should service themselves – the Church saw itself as the appropriate provider. This acted to curtail state involvement and was no doubt associated with the growth of what has turned out to be quite a vibrant voluntary sector. Today there are many voluntary organisations involved in service provision in Ireland. The model of development of Irish social policy provision has been quite specific: usually voluntary organisations have tended to pioneer the provision of different services with the state then becoming involved at a later stage (Curry, 1993, p. 172).

Hence the development of services for the family (and the elderly) was slow and limited to families in crisis or need. One of the most developed areas of service provision was that

Jutro (handwritten annotation)

of marriage and child counselling. Such services are still run by voluntary organisations, having been set up in the 1960s as church initiatives.

1.2 The Tradition of Family Policy in Ireland

Tradition implies the rooting and build-up of policies over the course of time. A thorough analysis of the tradition of family policy must identify the key actors behind developments, the, values and sets of norms and assumptions which they represent and the motives, objectives or stated intentions of (changes in) policy. The last section has considered the programmes and the legal architecture underlying family policy in Ireland. While this will inform the analysis of the tradition of family policy in Ireland, in this section specific attention is devoted to identifying the objectives and principles of policy as they have developed over the course of time as well as the main actors associated with the policy field.

The objectives of policy in Ireland, especially income support policy, as it related to the family were closely linked to the avoidance of poverty. It was recognised that children may place families under financial pressure and so the children's allowances were introduced to alleviate such pressures. Policy on the family in Ireland, then, started with families with children. A second and related objective was to support the family as an institution. A particular form of the family was supported, the family founded on marriage. This was inscribed especially in the taxation provisions for married couples.

In terms of influences, the debate in the UK exerted quite an important influence as did the strong anti-poverty orientation of the social policy architecture which Ireland inherited from that country. But, early policy on the family in Ireland was guided as much by negative constraints as by what might be said to be positive motives. Hence, strict limits were placed on the scope of family-related policies and the line of their development was incrementalist and gradual rather than experimental and expansionist. There are many examples of 'policy caution' – the limiting of children's allowances when they were first introduced to third and subsequent children, situating provision for lone mothers in social assistance rather than social insurance. Taking an overview, it is hard to disagree with McLaughlin (1993, p. 210) that the ideologies governing social policy sought to ensure that the family took primary responsibility for its own welfare. This fitted well with the general principles which defined social welfare provision in Ireland at the time: flat-rate, subsidiary, selective benefits paid to very particular (and sometimes small) sectors of the population. One can, therefore, trace much of the form of social protection in Ireland to a basic position on the family. Flat-rate social insurance was attractive because it would not undermine the husband/father's primary responsibility to provide for his family through his own industry and endeavour.

Fahey (1998) convincingly demonstrates that family policy in Ireland has its roots as much in the strong support of family farming in the early decades of the life of the state as in measures to directly affect the wellbeing and form of families. However there are different ways of characterising the approach taken to the family in Ireland. Working with the concept of policy paradigm,[10] Fahey is of the view that Irish policy on the family has been shaped by two contrasting sets of principles. The first, what he calls 'patriarchal familism', prevailed until the 1960s when it was superseded although not replaced by the second, what he terms 'egalitarian individualism'. Patriarchal familism treats the family as a mini-community which operates according to altruistic and solidaristic (as distinct from individualistic) principles. The type of family it promotes is a familiar one in Ireland: based on distinct roles for women and men and a hierarchical line of authority in which the husband/father is the head of the family and the needs of women and children take second place to those of men. This kind of family is located in a social context where values, policies and laws treat internal family relations as private. In this paradigm, the nature of state activity around the family is circumscribed and, as Fahey points out, strains of anti-statism are to be found. What the latter means is that when it comes to the family the motives of the state are treated with some suspicion. In fact, the very definition of the 'private' nature of the family derives its meaning from an absence of state intervention.

According to Fahey, this type of family policy began to give way sometime in the late 1960s or thereafter to a philosophy informed by the principles of individualism and egalitarianism. Combining these leads Fahey to depict the second stage of family policy in Ireland as founded on individual rights which were not contingent on one's sex or family status. Policy in this mode facilitates choice in personal behaviour and shows a concern for the rights of individuals rather than protection of the family as a unit. While it may be too extreme to claim that the 'black box' of the family is opened up, there is a greater recognition that social policy in the past supported inegalitarian relations within families, with sometimes negative consequences for women and children. The move to give benefits to unmarried mothers, to pay the children's allowances to the mother, and the general consolidation of social insurance could be taken as evidence of a movement towards egalitarian individualism. Whether the picture is quite as Fahey represents it is another matter.

Fahey's characterisation of the second phase of Irish family policy is questionable on a number of grounds. One of the main problems is his depiction of it in terms of egalitarian individualism. Fahey never defines this nor does he consider or discuss just how the two principles of egalitarianism and individualism, in themselves very complex, come together in Irish social policy. His analysis almost assumes that they are synonymous. But this is not the case – in effect there are many varieties of both individualism and egalitarianism and so a possible union of the two is by no means straightforward. In addition, the egalitarian dimension of policy in Ireland was slower to develop than Fahey suggests. It is difficult to read the creation of a specific benefit for lone mothers as signalling a move towards either egalitarianism or individualism. One could, for example, see it as an anti-abortion measure; it is certainly pro-family (albeit a different kind of family). Furthermore, the extent to which it could be characterised as a move towards individualism is questionable since women receive the payment only in their role as mothers (and hence not as individuals). Fahey may be wrong about the periodisation also – the 1960s-1970s is too early to locate such a fundamental change. Among other things it leaves him with no means to characterise the very significant developments in family policy which flooded the late 1990s.

Knowing who the key actors are is also vital to the analysis of policy, not just to locate the measure but because actors are associated with particular sets of interests. For Ireland it is relatively easy to piece together the story of the agency underlying family policy over time. The state and the Catholic church were the two predominant architects of Irish family policy. State action was sometimes spearheaded by the civil service, sometimes by the legislature and always by a government on a time-limited term of office. It was however substantial. As Fahey (1998, p. 400) points out, the strong role played by the state in promoting certain models of family life was a persistent feature of state-family relations in Ireland throughout the twentieth century.

The other great actor in Irish social policy was the Catholic Church. The Catholic influence in Irish social policy is not however by any means unidimensional or simplistic. The principle of subsidiarity is a towering influence. This idea, propounded in the papal encyclical *Quadragesimo Anno* (of 1931), determines the role of the state and other social institutions in the development and wellbeing of individuals. A form of 'no go area' is declared between the family and the state, as individuals and families must be (enabled to be) self-sufficient. This means a secondary or background role for social policy, background that is to the family, self-help and private provision.[11] Individual, family and community responsibility were emphasised (McLaughlin, 1993). This principle and the generally strong influence of Catholic ideology on Irish social policy left a very particular mark on social service provision, among other things. But Catholicism alone is incomplete as an explanation of the development of policy on the family in Ireland. For McLaughlin (1993) and Fahey (1998) are correct to point out that Irish nationalism

and Catholicism concurred on the appropriate roles and
relations of the family and the state (among other things).
McLaughlin (1993, pp. 208-210) suggests that middle class
nationalists were averse to paying high taxes and that there
was a receptivity, in the early period in the life of the state
anyway, to *laissez-faire* economic policies.

1.3 Some Critical Aspects of Irish Policy on the Family

In some ways it took a long time for the notion of family as a
general concept to make its way into Irish social policy. The
categorical approach that dominated social policy historically
meant that families were viewed in quite particular terms.
Since the inception of the state, family policy equalled
income provision for children and for some individuals in
their family roles (e.g. widows). This approach was even
visible in deliberations about reform. For example, the
Commission on Social Welfare (1986), one of the few, and
arguably the largest, review exercises ever carried out on Irish
social policy, had no general conception either of family or
family policy. To the extent that it used the term at all, family
was a specific category (as in lone-parent families). The
Commission operated throughout its deliberations with parts
of families or demographic categories: children, couples,
single adults, young persons aged sixteen to eighteen years,
and so forth. It nowhere put them together to consider
measures for the welfare of the family as a collective unit. It
viewed the problems in Irish social policy in terms of the
failure to develop provision according to a set of fundamental
principles. The Commission set out the following as its
principles for Irish social policy: adequacy, redistribution,
comprehensiveness, consistency and simplicity. It never
made sufficiently clear how these principles should be
applied to provision for individuals as against provision for
families.

To the extent that the welfare of children was an issue
historically in Ireland, it was the wellbeing of children who
did not have access to a 'normal' family that was the main
concern. Child wellbeing was seen to be coterminous with
living in the family of origin. The benevolence of parental and

other family relationships went more or less unquestioned until the 1990s. Not only was there a tendency to romanticise the family but the depiction and treatment of it as a private sphere brought a reluctance to look inside the family. While this view of the family prevailed almost everywhere at some point in time, it persisted in Ireland for longer than it did in other European countries.

Up to the early 1990s, it is striking that the objectives of policy in relation to the family in Ireland are nowhere clearly stated. It was not until the Interim Report of the Commission on the Family in 1996 that the country had an official presentation on the principles and objectives of family policy. Following this, the Social Inclusion Strategy produced by the Interdepartmental Committee monitoring the National Anti-Poverty Strategy drew attention to key issues for the family. These included income adequacy, the employment effects of child income support, the needs of one-parent families and family incentives.

A second possible criticism is that Irish social policy was, if not out of touch with, then certainly a laggard in relation to developments in the wider society. It was not until the mid-1980s that the assumption of a wife's economic dependency on her husband was formally addressed, for example. Prior to that social welfare payments, in form and entitlement, endorsed a strong variant of the male breadwinner/housewife model of family. Montanari's (2000, p. 232) analysis shows that Ireland consistently favoured marriage subsidies through the tax system rather than child benefits as a form of family support between 1950 and 1990. In an international perspective, Ireland was unusual in this regard, one of only five countries to do so (in the 1950-1970 period along with Denmark, Germany and Japan and in the 1975-1990 period with Australia, Denmark and the USA). In the latter period, the gap between the marriage subsidy and the child benefit was very large in Ireland.

Developments in other countries will now be examined so as to give an idea of how Irish family policy compares with that in other countries.

Chapter 2

The Origins and Development of Family Policy in Europe

Comparison has many advantages for learning. In this chapter the development of family policy in Ireland up to 1990 is placed in a broader European context. Note that the review in this chapter is not limited to the four European countries which along with Ireland are the focus of this research overall. When it comes to the earlier development of family policy, a wider comparison is very insightful. A number of questions guided this analysis: Is Ireland's historical trajectory similar or different to that of other countries? To what extent do the actors and objectives of family policy resemble those found elsewhere? Is Ireland a larger or smaller spender on family policy relative to other countries?

2.1 The Origins of Family Policy in Europe

The term 'family policy' took a long time to mature. According to Gauthier (1996, pp. 158-159) the term was little used until the mid-1970s. Thereafter, its use became more widespread. It is certainly true that family policy started small. It was also quite contentious.

According to Wennemo (1994, p. 19), debates about family policy in the first decades of the twentieth century had strong moral currents. There was a perceived conflict between two potential goals of family policy: improving the living conditions of needy families and raising moral standards in society. It was recognised more or less from the outset that, because family measures create incentives for different types of behaviour, especially around intimate relationships and fertility, they contain moral hazards. Helping needy families was therefore not straightforward. By doing so one was running the risk of endorsing behaviour and life styles that were regarded as potentially unsocial; the most needy families were then, as now, families reared by women on their own, those headed by men out of work and those with large numbers of children. Drawing upon the then prevailing ideology about deserving and undeserving poor – which deemed some categories of the population more deserving of public support than others – the cause of a family's need was very important. If families were perceived to be in need through no fault of their own, then they were more likely to be regarded as deserving of support from the public purse. Closely related to this moral dimension was a concern about the incentive effects of introducing measures to support families. Policy makers did not want to encourage men or women to be irresponsible about their family obligations. A somewhat different, and generally positive, view was taken of state support for families with many children (Wennemo, 1994, p. 23). These families were generally considered as being 'responsible' and a high regard was placed on them in some countries, such as France, where pro-natalist ideas were very influential. Large family size would also find favour with Catholic philosophy which saw it as part of men and women's duty to bear and rear children. English-speaking countries were not unduly concerned about population growth. Rather, the questions which dominated there focused on moral concerns such as which parents ought to (be allowed to) have the largest numbers of children. Fertility rates across different social classes were often a source of concern since in most countries it was the poorer classes that had the largest families.

Wennemo (1994) suggests not only that family types were treated differently but that one can actually read how they were ranked from the development and growth of family support measures. One group, the support of which nowhere met with much opposition, was widows with dependent children. Provision for these families was the first form of family support measure introduced in a number of countries, for example in the USA, Denmark and Canada as early as 1911, 1913 and 1916 (respectively). Another group seen as deserving were families with disabled fathers or mothers. Opinion was more divided about large families. In countries where pro-natalism was important, for example France, these were among the first families to benefit from public support (as early as 1913). However, benefits for such families can also stem from an anti-poverty orientation, as in Ireland, New Zealand and the UK. The most problematic group of families for policy purposes consisted of those headed by divorced, deserted and unmarried mothers. The perceived moral risk in supporting these women, especially unmarried mothers, lay in the possibility of encouraging them to bear more children and to permit irresponsibility on the part of the children's fathers. The Scandinavian countries, Sweden especially, seemed to be less concerned about this possible effect. Their policies tended not to differentiate between married and unmarried mothers. France is also notable in this respect in that the benefit which it introduced for larger families in 1913 was actually increased if the family was headed by a single mother.[12]

It seems, then, that most countries attached conditions to their early family benefits in order to guard against moral laxity and economic disincentives. A variety of conditions was employed: means tests, either increasing or reducing the benefit for larger families, excluding parents who were not economically active, directing tax deductions at families with the highest incomes. All of these, as Wennemo (1994, p. 25) points out, are methods for decreasing the incentives for the poor to have many children. In most countries, the first family benefits were directed at special categories of families.

Yet there are common patterns to be found (Bahle, 1995). Countries resembled each other in how they developed their first family benefits; indeed some tended to follow each other's approach. One can identify three general patterns in regard to the adoption and early development of cash benefits for families with children in Europe.

1. The first prevailed in the continental European countries, Austria, Belgium, Italy, the Netherlands and Switzerland especially. In these countries benefits were tied to employment and paid usually by employers as part of the wage to the father. The patriarchal family was the focus of policy, with the breadwinner role of men receiving support largely, so that married women would not be compelled into employment. Large families were also supported and single mothers disadvantaged.

2. The Scandinavian countries took a different approach. They tended to be relatively early in introducing family benefits and they also tended towards a more universalistic approach, loath to differentiate among mothers on the basis of marital status. In direct contrast to the continental European countries, the economic wellbeing of children of unmarried mothers, of which there were many, was a special concern of early family support policy in the Scandinavian countries.

3. The English-speaking countries, which formed the third pattern, are not so easy to classify. However, they tended to have been rather moralistic and to have made a differentiation between different types of families, with the marital status of the parents being especially important for this purpose. The UK initiated its family policy with benefits for widows and orphans in 1925 but did not take any further action until 1944 when it introduced child benefits. The USA and Canada were to the forefront in introducing pensions for single mothers. Admittedly, the mothers had to undergo tests of means and morals and widows were favoured, but the role of the USA as an early innovator in family policy is remarkably at odds with the subsequent (under)development of social policy there.

It is important to note that Ireland is not so easily placed in these international patterns. It differed from other English-speaking countries in that large families were not generally the focus of early family support measures in those countries

(Wennemo, 1994, p. 43). However, Ireland was similar to other countries in that widows were a main focus of early policy interest, with a generally punitive attitude taken to unmarried mothers. Its concern about child poverty levels, however, meant that Ireland resembled Britain as well as the Scandinavian countries.

Before and after the Second World War is a good benchmark for policy on the family, with the post-war period especially heralding a move to a more universal approach in Europe. The USA is alone among the developed countries in failing to introduce a system of family support. It is also marked by a continuing concern about the moral implications of supporting families with children, especially those headed by a woman on her own. Elsewhere, as benefits became universalised, moral questions became less relevant (although they have re-emerged in the last decade or so in some countries such as the UK). Across postwar Europe, support to families was no longer regarded either as a woman-specific question or as a population question (Wennemo, 1994, p. 40). Another reason for the move to universalism was that resources became available when the costs of war dropped – taxes had been increased during the war but once it was over extra resources were available at no additional cost to the tax payer.

2.2 Some Characteristics of Family Policy

Gauthier (1996, p. 196) suggests that what is today referred to as family policy is the result of a long development, starting with limited measures aimed at protecting mothers and children and moving, sometimes gradually, to a comprehensive package of cash and in-kind benefits aimed at all families. As it developed in Europe, family policy came to be characterised by certain particularities. Many of these are also to be found in Ireland. Most European countries have supported the family by developing particular sets of cash benefits for families within their general social security systems. These tend to be 'add-ons' and as such have usually had some distinct features. Child benefits, for example, tend to be unique among cash transfers in that they are the only universal measures in most welfare states (including Ireland). At the time of their introduction, and subsequently, they represented a truly innovative form of social right since they involve no conditions for receipt (Montanari, 2000, p. 309). In addition, many cash payments for families were introduced by reforming key principles of social insurance (Bieback, 1992, p. 243). In fact there is some evidence that state support for families constitutes a separate domain of social policy within and across nations (Gauthier, 1999). Another way in which they are specific is that the periods of the expansion and retraction of family benefits do not generally conform to more general trends in the development of welfare state benefits. For example, family benefits were introduced later than social insurance – by 1945 only a quarter of the eighteen most developed countries had introduced family benefits (Wennemo, 1994, p. 61). Furthermore, the growth that took place in cash benefits for families after the Second World War was much more modest than that of other components of the welfare state which expanded rapidly (although not in Ireland). Similarly, family benefits have generally been less affected than other benefits by the cut-backs and retrenchment of benefits which took root in Europe in the 1990s.

Closely related to the diversity in the form of policy is variation in the motives for introducing support for families. The most long-standing and established of these are pro-natalism, horizontal redistribution, poverty prevention, the education and wellbeing of children and the encouragement of particular family forms (especially the breadwinner family where the husband/father is employed and the wife/mother works full-time in the home). A concern about mothers' income is also to be found in the debates about family support. This has broadened over the years to a concern about gender inequalities but in the early years it was mainly about mothers having some independent income. In this spirit, Sweden and the UK paid the children's allowances to the mother from the outset. In comparison, Irish family policy was historically quite unidimensional and remained generally unconcerned about gender and intra-familial issues until the 1970s.

2.3 Similarities and Differences between Ireland and Other Countries

One can, taking an overview, identify a number of ways in which Ireland's historical trajectory resembles that of other countries. Family support systems in most countries have their roots in poverty and poor relief (Wennemo, 1994, p. 8). Nor is Ireland all that unusual either in the timing of its supports for families.[13] Family allowances were introduced in Europe between 1930 and 1956 with most activity occurring in the 1930s and 1940s (Gauthier, 1999, p. 945). It was also normal practice for the early benefits to be selective, excluding some categories of families with children. Selectivity fell by the wayside over time, just as it did in Ireland. However, this trend towards universality was partially reversed in Europe in the late 1980s and early 1990s (Wennemo, 1994, p. 5). Finally, Ireland is not unusual in the fact that its family policies consist of an amalgam of measures (Gauthier, 1996). However, Ireland differs from other countries in a number of respects as well.

A first source of variation is the generosity of support. When the value of payments between 1949 and 1990 is compared to that elsewhere, Ireland is consistently among the least generous supporters of families (Table 1). In the forty years covered by the table, Ireland's cash benefits for a two-child family never exceeded 3 per cent of the average wage in manufacturing industry. Despite some changes in the 1970s, one could accurately summarise Ireland's historical pattern of cash support for families with children as being consistently low, although over time on an upward curve. As will be clear from later sections of this report, this curve took a sharply upward turn in the second half of the 1990s. Indeed, by the year 2001, cash benefits for families were equivalent to 7.7 per cent of the average wage of male industrial workers in manufacturing.

Historically, however, Ireland has been a laggard. The only countries that paid less than Ireland in 1961 were Denmark and Germany; in 1970 no country paid lower family allowances than Ireland; in 1980 only Spain paid less and in 1990 Ireland was ahead of only Spain and Italy. Comparison, then, shows Ireland to have had most in common with the Mediterranean countries. Its consistency in terms of the (low) level of support also separates Ireland from most other countries that tended to vary their level of support from period to period. While this variation makes it difficult to judge the most generous providers, generally Austria, Belgium, Luxembourg and, less consistently so, France and the Netherlands have paid the most generous cash benefits to families with children. Italy is probably the least consistent country in that by 1990 it had no universal cash benefit in operation whereas in 1961 it was the most generous country for families with children.

A second difference between Ireland and many other countries is in the degree of diversity of its family support. With four basic forms of support – child benefit, child dependant allowances, Family Income Supplement and tax allowances (up to 1986) – Ireland operated a more diverse support package for families than most of its European neighbours (though it closely resembled policy in the UK). Note however that while it could claim to be diverse in its income programmes for families with children, these more or less comprised the entirety of Irish family policy. This brings up the third particularity of Ireland – the underdeveloped nature of its service provision (for families and in general). It was not just that the state provided few services for families – state provision of services was unpopular also in other countries (such as Germany) – but rather that few family services were provided at all. The reference here is not just to the absence of childcare but also to the lack of a range of community-based services for care of the elderly and the general absence of a supportive service infrastructure for families in need. Fourthly, Ireland was unusual also in that it did not have the moral debates about supporting families in anything like the depth which took place elsewhere. In some ways this was due to the prominence of the Catholic Church. The situation was that matters which occasioned vigorous debate elsewhere were either not raised or raised in a manner in which the appropriate courses of action were set out as more or less self-evident. Finally, it is worth pointing out that family policy in Ireland was not overlaid with the very strong pro-natalist concerns and interests prevailing elsewhere in Europe.

Table 1:   *Generosity of Cash Supports for Families with Children 1949-1997**

Country	1949	1961	1970	1980	1990	1997
Austria	5.3	10.3	10.8	13.0	11.3	9.6
Belgium	11.2	16.5	13.5	9.8	10.4	7.5
Denmark	0.0	0.0	6.4	3.4	5.2	7.3
Finland	7.1	6.2	4.3	5.4	6.2	10.7
France	18.7	13.2	7.5	5.2	7.1	13.6
Germany	0.0	0.0	2.2	4.9	4.9	9.1
Greece	0.0	7.1	8.4	6.8	3.2	1.1
Ireland	0.0	2.0	2.2	2.5	3.0	4.4
Italy	16.8	21.5	10.1	4.6	0.0	0.0
Luxembourg	10.0	11.9	7.8	7.2	8.3	10.3
Netherlands	10.4	10.0	9.4	8.6	7.4	7.2
Norway	2.8	2.5	5.2	6.4	9.1	9.0
Portugal	0.0	20.2	10.7	3.8	4.9	5.9
Spain	2.7	2.2	5.6	1.0	0.3	0.0
Sweden	9.6	6.4	6.1	6.6	7.2	6.3
Switzerland	0.0	4.5	2.4	3.8	4.7	7.3
UK	3.9	2.9	3.5	8.9	6.3	5.5

Source: Adapted from Gauthier (1999), Table 2, p. 948.
*   Measured on the basis of cash allowances to a two-child family calculated as a percentage of the average male wage in manufacturing.

2.4 Classifying Countries on their Family Policy

When it comes to comparing countries, it is helpful to organise the similarities and differences in terms of a policy model and to investigate the extent to which policy models vary across countries. This helps both to reduce the amount of variation and to reveal the architecture of different forms of provision. A major point of discussion in the literature, especially the comparative scholarship, is the extent to which an articulated family policy can be said to exist and what variations there are on that across nations. This essentially draws on the coherence of family policy and whether a policy focusing specifically on the family (rather than family policy by default) exists. This kind of framework has been used to produce different classifications of countries (which is a key objective of comparative research). One of the first cross-national comparisons – a study by Kamerman and Kahn (1978) which did not include Ireland – classified the family policies of fourteen countries into three groups:

1. those with an explicit and comprehensive family policy;
2. those with family policy as a field extending across various policy domains;
3. countries where family policies were implicit and reluctant.

Underlying this clustering of countries is a continuum whereby family policies are implicit or explicit, comprehensive or episodic, harmonised or uncoordinated (Fox Harding, 1996, p. 205). However, Gauthier's work shows that different components of family policies do not necessarily form an integrated whole, judged in terms of the nature, direction and timing of reform. Hence, she points out that Denmark, Germany and Norway saw the largest increases in cash benefits between 1950 and 1997 while Finland, Norway and Sweden experienced the most generous increase in maternity benefits (Gauthier, 1999, p. 960). Norway is the only country of the seventeen considered which saw large increases in both forms of state support for families. She also notes that no clear clusters of countries emerge from her analysis.

There are other approaches to classifying family policy (Bundesministerium für Familie und Senioren, 1993). Fox Harding (1996, p. 177), for example, focuses on the family-state relation and views it as having (at least) two dimensions: control and support. She suggests a series of models of the family-state relationship varying on a continuum whereby state policies are highly controlling and proactive to those which are highly reactive.[14] While she does not apply these models across countries, she does offer a detailed account of how they compare with one another. Fox Harding sees five such models of policy:

1. the enforcement of family responsibilities in certain domains;

2. the manipulation of incentives in order to create specific family behaviours and forms;

3. the use of constraining assumptions which limit the boundaries of family variation;

4. substituting for or supporting those roles which are normally carried out in families;

5. responding to needs and demands as they arise from families.

The first three models tend to emphasise duties and obligations for the family. In identifying them, the sanctions and degree of surveillance and monitoring at the disposition of the state to ensure compliance are very important. Rewards, especially economic incentives, are also important because underlying most policies is a structure of incentives which rewards certain kinds of behaviour and penalises others (Fox Harding, p. 189). The third model, which focuses on policy as a set of assumptions, is intended to take account of the situation where a country may have no explicit family policy or no agreed set of goals or objectives in relation to the family. In this scenario, policy may tilt the balance of advantages in a particular direction but it is not so directive as to actively prohibit or penalise particular behaviours (Fox Harding, p. 192). In the fourth and fifth models, the state more or less works with existing patterns by supporting families, responding to their needs and stepping in with an alternative (only) when they are in trouble. These vary from the other models in that the initiative is either shared between family and state or in the fifth type of model lies primarily with the family. In this kind of scenario, people may be treated more as individuals than as family members. As models they are both more open about and more responsive to the kind of family change that is desirable.

While, as mentioned above, Fox Harding does not apply these to particular countries, they are helpful because they draw attention to the prescriptive elements or effects of policy. The reality is that family policy, like all other policy areas, circumscribes behaviour and sets out an incentive structure for particular courses of action over others.

2.5 Explaining Patterns of Family Policy

When it comes to explaining cross-national patterning, there are a number of theoretical perspectives. Among these, arguments around economic development, politics and the mobilisation of women are especially relevant.

The first of these explanations draws on a thesis about industrialisation. Its logic of argumentation in relation to social policy rests on the case that as societies develop they have on the one hand a greater need of social policy and on the other hand more resources to devote to it. In this evolutionist model, all developed societies have social policies which are both necessary to development and also a consequence of it. An underlying part of its logic is that social policy is almost inevitable and that developed societies become progressively more like each other. When applied to the realm of family policy, this explanation regards changes in the needs of families and in families' environments as the driving force behind governments' family policies (Gauthier, 1996, p. 4). A particular variant of this approach concentrates on the economics of children and associated fertility patterns. In this framework, state support for families with children may influence the demand for children by reducing the cost of having and rearing children or by increasing household income. Very little is known about trends over time in the direct costs of children but the indirect (or opportunity) costs of children are known to have strongly increased since the 1960s. This is because rising wages for women's employment increase the potential loss to the family if the wife or mother is not in employment. In this kind of scenario, one can assume an increase in state support to families. Ireland has historically sought to assist families with the direct costs of children. However at the present time, the country is in the grip of a debate about how families should be supported in the context of the increasing opportunity or indirect costs of children as employment has expanded and women's paid labour is needed in the work force (to be discussed in subsequent chapters).

The second theory is political in origin and is related to the determinants of the welfare state and family benefits and especially to a society's preference for children. Trade unions and political parties of the left are assumed to be in favour of welfare state expansion because it gives workers a cushion against a harsh and unpredictable economy. Although trade unions across Europe have tended to be ambivalent about family benefits – because they may be used as arguments against increasing wages – they generally tend to support measures that involve redistribution. Strong trade unions and left-wing political parties are therefore assumed to be associated with high levels of state support for families (Wennemo, 1994). The strength of religious parties is also seen to be a factor leading to more generous family benefits. These parties, especially influenced by Catholicism, tend to see it as the state's duty to protect families. Ireland's history is somewhat different in this respect in that: (a) it never had an overtly religious party, and (b) the version of Catholicism which prevailed in Ireland was resistant to state intervention in relation to the family (Daly, 1999). The political party explanation does not go very far in Ireland for another reason: parties do not differ very much from each other either on their position on social policy in general or family policy in particular.

The political engagement of women and their presence in the labour force is another relevant factor utilised to explain the development of family benefits. Gauthier (1996), for example, found that the development of maternity-related leave and benefits from the 1960s was closely linked in the developed countries to the level of female participation in the labour force. Wennemo's analysis of eighteen OECD countries showed that the political strength of women (as indicated by the timing of female suffrage) and the existence of religious parties were the two most significant factors behind differences in the early family policy initiatives (1994, p. 45). Again Ireland does not fit so readily into this explanatory framework. However if one disaggregates the gender variable into political mobilisation and women's presence in the labour force, then the low level of the latter might serve to explain why Ireland's support of the family was on the meagre side. There is no doubt but that, when women are needed in the labour market, national policy galvinises in regard to family measures in general and childcare provision in particular. Since Ireland's economy only very gradually became open to employing women in large numbers, this was not the motor of policy development in Ireland that it was elsewhere.

How is the pattern of family support which has been built up over time being reformed in Ireland and elsewhere? The next chapter considers developments in Ireland during the 1990s, whereas Chapter 4 will examine reforms in other countries and considers how development in Ireland compares.

Chapter 3

Development and Reform in Family Policy in Ireland in the 1990s

Because of the way in which social welfare systems in Ireland and elsewhere have developed in the last ten to fifteen years, some new categories have to be introduced for the analysis of family policy in recent years as against earlier periods. Considerations which have appeared on the policy landscape in Ireland in the last ten to fifteen years include gender equity, the labour force participation patterns of parents and of younger family members, and the welfare and care mix. Hence, in addition to the more familiar categories of benefits for families with children, three new categories of analysis have to be added. The first is that of policies to reconcile work and family life, the second is policies on care and the third is general family support services.

Policies to reconcile work and family life are essentially oriented to facilitating employment of mothers but they are also informed by a concern to valorise family activities and family life in general. In a Europe-wide context, they are rather new. While many countries have been concerned to facilitate mothers' employment, most have either valued employment over family for both women and men (e.g. Scandinavia) or have differentiated on gender grounds, valuing stay-at-home motherhood for women and employment for men (especially true of the continental European countries). The emergence of reconciliation of work and family life as a policy concern on the part of the EU has been very significant in raising the profile of this issue on the policy agenda at national level.

The second new category to be added is that of care. This concept, focusing on the wellbeing of children as well as that of ill and elderly adults, is increasingly used in social policy analysis to capture a growing field of welfare state activity. Care refers to the activities involved in caring for children and ill, elderly or handicapped adults and the economic, normative and social contexts within which these activities are carried out (Daly and Lewis, 1998, p. 6). As a concept, care emerged from the feminist literature and, while it was originally used to gain recognition for these activities as work, it has now come to refer more to the emotional as well as material aspects of the relationship between the person who provides the care (care giver) and he or she who receives it (care receiver). As women enter the labour force in ever larger numbers and family ties no longer spell a readiness to care personally for parents and elderly relatives, welfare states have had to become more active in providing either cash benefits or services for the young and old in need of care. This has provided the impetus for a change in the objectives, and in some cases the substance, of family policy.

Family support services is an arena of policy that has been gaining increasing attention in recent years, both in Ireland and elsewhere. Generally aimed at supporting families in carrying out their 'functions', family support services usually involve counselling, guidance, education and/or advice. Their development has been closely linked to a renewed emphasis on parental responsibilities, which was reinforced, inter alia, in the UN Convention on the Rights of the Child. In Ireland, family support services have traditionally been a very under-developed area of welfare state provision. However, since the report of the Commission on the Family recommended their development in 1998, there has been a lot of policy activity in this area.

The second half of the 1990s was a very active period in Irish social policy. It was as if the lifting of financial constraints, itself occasioned by the massive economic boom experienced by Ireland in that period, opened the floodgates of opportunity. The family was at the centre of policy activity. Indeed all the major social policy reviews undertaken during the decade related in one way or another to the family.

3.1 Changes in Policy in the 1990s

The policy context in Ireland was more or less redefined during the 1990s. Indeed we shall probably look back on the decade as a watershed. Two, not unrelated, factors were responsible: the increasingly positive state of the public finances and the evolution of a consensus-based social partnership model of national planning. As is well known, Ireland's rate of economic and employment growth from the mid-1990s to 2001 surpassed both expectations and European standards and led to considerable increases in the average standard of living. From the early 1990s on, economic buoyancy and public finance surpluses gave government more leeway in social policy than it had ever before experienced. On some occasions the Irish government was searching for areas in which to invest while its counterparts elsewhere in Europe were looking for potential budget cuts. One can see the changing economic environment reflected in the realm of social policy – the early 1990s saw little if any change whereas from about the middle of the decade on innovation and reform were much more common. The second element – social partnership – is equally significant for social policy. As partnership grew, the management of the economy, and in some respects society, came to be governed in a highly consensual fashion. Since the mid-1980s, the government, employers, farmers and trade unions, joined later by representatives of the voluntary and community sectors, have engaged in a process whereby the inputs to economic and social growth, as well as the distribution of some of the outputs, were subject to negotiation and a public planning process. The current three-year programme is the fifth national agreement in Ireland since 1987. With the gradual inclusion over time of representatives of the community sector and the unemployed and the establishment of a national consultative social forum, partnership in Ireland is assuming a strong social face. The national programme is far more than an agreement about wages and wage setting.

Rather, it assumes the character of a national plan with a strong social orientation. However, the high degree of consensus prevailing throughout the 1990s has started to show cracks. Although a new three-year national agreement was negotiated in mid-2000, there has been considerable industrial unrest, especially among public sector workers. This has placed the social partnership process under increasing pressure.

In terms of social policy generally, the most significant measure associated with national planning was the anti-poverty process which was first put in place in 1997. The National Anti-Poverty Strategy is little more than mentioned in this report because it did not prioritise family matters as such. For the present purposes therefore, it is more background than foreground. The social planning process did, however, realise some of its effects, especially in the later years of the decade, in significant increases in the levels of social welfare benefits. Against a discourse of equality and social justice, social welfare recipients and low-waged workers were targeted for larger than average increases in benefits. Family policy was also the subject of significant reform. The main developments in policy relevant to the family which were effected in the 1990s will now be described.

3.1.1 Changes in Cash Benefits for Families with Children

3.1.1.1 Child Benefits

Having languished for much of the late 1980s and early 1990s, in recent years the universal child benefit has been the channel through which support for families has been increased and altered. Child benefits were targeted for expansion from the mid-1990s on (Table 2). Each of the six years between 1996 and 2001 saw increases in the level of the benefit.

The scale of the increases was generally progressive from year to year, culminating in an average increase of some 56 per cent in 2001. As a result, child benefit rates were about four times higher in 2001 than they had been in 1990, with an increase of 327 per cent over the decade. Child benefit is

*Table 2:   Main Developments in Cash Benefits for Families
          in Ireland 1990-2001*

Year	Child Benefits (CB)	Child Dependant Allowances (CDAs)	Family Income Supplement (FIS)
1990	Lower rate (1st to 4th child) increased from €19.1 to €20 and higher rate (5th +) from €27.6 to €29	Minimum rate of CDAs fixed at €13.9. Entitlement extended to children aged 20 yrs in full-time education	Income limits increased. Receipt of FIS no longer affects a family's entitlement to medical card. Workers who expect to work for at least 6 months made eligible
1991	Rates for 4th child brought to the higher rate of €29	Minimum rate fixed at €15.2. Rationalisation of CDAs from 6 rates to 3. Entitlement extended to those aged 21 in full-time education	Extension of Supplement to families with children aged 18-21 in full-time education. Improvements in income limits. Scheme extended to cohabiting couples with children
1992	-	-	Weekly income limits raised by €19
1993	Lower rates increased by 4.2%	Minimum rates increased from €15.2 to €16.2	Weekly income limits raised by €25.3. Rates improved
1994	Lower rates increased by 25% and higher rates by 8.6%	Minimum rates increased to €16.7	Weekly income limits raised by €12.6. Period over which weekly family earnings calculated reduced from 6 to 4 weeks

Table 2: **Main Developments in Cash Benefits for Families in Ireland 1990-2001 (Continued)**

Year	Child Benefits (CB)	Child Dependant Allowances (CDAs)	Family Income Supplement (FIS)
1995	Rates for third child brought to higher rates. Lower and higher rates increased by €8.8, representing an av. increase of about 32%	CDA rates frozen	Weekly income limits raised by between €7.6 and €16.5 (depending on family size). Increases in payment rates. Introduction of a minimum payment of €6.3 a week. Reduction from 12 to 6 months in the length of time for which people must expect to be employed
1996	CB increased by €2.5 representing an av. increase of 7%	13 week retention of CDAs for people who, having been unemployed for 12 months or more and in receipt of full-rate CDA, take up employment for 4 weeks or more	Weekly income limits raised by €12.6. Qualifying employment period reduced from 6 to 3 months. Minimum working hours reduced from 20 per week to 38 per fortnight. FIS made available to job sharers
1997	Higher rate increased by €6.3 while lower rate increased by €1.2, representing an av. increase of 9%	13 week retention of CDAs for social welfare recipients taking up employment following a Community Employment Scheme or under the Jobs Initiative Scheme	Weekly income limits raised by €12.6. Method of calculating amount of FIS changed from gross income to net of PRSI contributions and health and employment levies

Table 2:   *Main Developments in Cash Benefits for Families*
           in Ireland 1990-2001 (Continued)

Year	Child Benefits (CB)	Child Dependant Allowances (CDAs)	Family Income Supplement (FIS)
1998	Higher rate increased by €3.8 while lower rate increased by €1.9, representing an av. increase of 6%	-	Weekly income limits raised by €8.8. Method of calculating amount of FIS changed to net income (pay after tax, levies and superannuation)
1999	Higher rate increased by €5 and lower rate by €3.8, representing an av. increase of 9.5%	-	Weekly income limits raised by €10.1
2000	Higher rate increased by €12.6 and lower rate by €10.1, representing an av. increase of 22%	Full CDAs paid when spouse earns up to €171.4 a week (previously CDAs were paid at half rate once €76 exceeded)	Weekly income limits raised by €16.5
2001	Higher rate increased by €31.7, lower rate by €38, representing an av. Increase of 56%	CDAs extended to cover children in education up to age 22. Upper ceiling of weekly earnings for full retention of CDAs increased to €184	Weekly income Limits raised by €31.7

attractive to Irish policy makers because it benefits all
children and is neutral as regards the employment status of
the mother (which is a very sensitive matter in Ireland). The
reduction of child poverty, by European standards relatively
high in Ireland, is another reason as to why families with
children are targeted for generous increases. The general
strategy of universal increases reflects additional concerns to

reduce poverty and unemployment traps and to move to a more integrated child income support system. This policy of improving the universal child benefit has however left the targeted benefits for children in low-income families more or less untouched in recent years.

3.1.1.2 Child Dependant Allowances

Child dependant allowances have seen a lot less policy activity than child benefits. As Plumb and Walsh (2000, p. 62) describe it, since 1994 the policy of enhancing child dependant allowances, which had followed on from the recommendations of the Commission on Social Welfare (1986), has come to a 'sudden halt'. Child dependant allowances represent an alternative approach to child benefit in that, since they are paid only to social welfare recipients, they are a targeted strategy. For the first five years of the 1990s, there were some increases in the rates of payment but these were small (more or less in line with general increases granted at that time). In 1991 the number of child dependant allowances was rationalised from six to three and the age limit was extended for children in education. Since 1995 these payments have been effectively frozen in value, policy makers having committed themselves to a more universal approach as described above. The main changes made relate to the possibility of retaining these payments for a period should benefit recipients take up employment (Table 2). From 1996 on, those taking up a job were allowed to retain their child dependant allowances for thirteen weeks; in 1997 this possibility was extended to recipients commencing a community employment scheme or availing of the jobs initiative scheme (i.e. welfare recipients entering employment). In 2000 this right was extended to the spouses of benefit recipients who are in employment and have earnings of up to €171 a week (previously the addition was reduced to a half rate when a weekly earnings threshold of €76 was reached). In 2001 the allowances were extended to cover 'children' in full-time education up to age twenty-two and the upper ceiling of weekly earnings for full retention of the benefit was increased from €171 to €184.

3.1.1.3 Family Income Supplement

The Family Income Supplement, Ireland's in-work benefit for low-earning families, has also seen many changes (Table 2). Consistent efforts have been made over the years to make the Supplement (and hence employment) more attractive and generous. Changes made include the introduction of a minimum payment, an increase in the multiplier (from 50 to 60 per cent of the gap between actual income and the ceiling, in 1989) and a reduction (in 1996) in the minimum hours worked from 20 a week to 38 a fortnight. In 1997 the method of calculating the payment changed from gross income to gross income less Pay Related Social Insurance (PRSI) and health and employment levy contributions. In 1998 the basis of the calculation of earnings was changed to net pay. During the decade, the weekly income thresholds for qualification for the supplement were reduced each year, usually by between €10 and €12.6. Again one can see this benefit becoming progressively more generous over the period – the increase in 2000 was €16.5 and in 2001 it was €32. Despite these changes, non-take up is estimated to be significant. However there is also significant growth in the numbers receiving the Supplement with an increase of 121 per cent throughout the decade. Statistics for the year 2000 show some 13,062 families receiving the Supplement (Department of Social, Community and Family Affairs, 2001).

In 1999 the general approach to subsidising low income from economic activity, as epitomised by the Family Income Supplement, was further extended in Irish social policy with the introduction of a new programme for low-income farmers. This new programme, entitled Farm Assist, is designed as an equivalent to the Family Income Supplement for low-income farmers. Some 14,000 farm families on low income qualify for this programme, which is an increase of some 7,000 on the numbers formerly in receipt of the special unemployment payment for farmers.

3.1.2 Financial Support for Lone Parent Families

The unmarried mother's allowance was integrated in 1990 with other social assistance payments for low-income women rearing children alone, to form a new Lone Parent's Allowance. This was significant in a number of respects, not least in that it represented a departure from the tradition for social policy in Ireland to differentiate between different (and sometimes very small) categories of women according to their marital or family situation. While the streamlining of provision for unmarried mothers, deserted wives, prisoners' wives and some widows may not appear revolutionary, it was a significant step away from the highly categorical, status-based character of income support policy in Ireland. Apart from its streamlining function, what was also significant about the Lone Parent's Allowance is that it signalled official recognition that men too are lone parents and are entitled to income support in that role should they need it.

Developments in provision for lone parents over the course of the 1990s could be characterised as broadening the conception of lone parent and facilitating their entry to the labour market. The year 1997 saw a further significant change in public policy on lone parents with the introduction of a more inclusive One-Parent Family Payment. Embodying a more employment-led approach also, this new payment sought to broaden the conception of lone parent to include the role of worker. It introduced certain enticements towards employment with earnings disregards (of €146 a week) which are among the most generous of any Irish social welfare payment.

3.1.3 Changes in Family-related Taxation

There is little sign of Ireland's pro-male breadwinner family income tax model being changed. The changes made in the 1990s tend to reinforce this type of model, although they have had as their main point of reference households in which parents are caring for children. There have been three main changes. In 1991, a tax allowance was introduced for widowed parents in the three years following the death of their spouse. In 1994-95 a new provision for the taxation of spouses was introduced, according to which either spouse can be nominated as the assessable person (prior to that, the husband was always the assessable person). This new measure was enacted following criticism of the taxation of married women by the Second Commission on the Status of Women (1993). The third change was perhaps the most significant measure: the introduction of the Home Carer's Allowance for the year 2000-2001. This is a tax allowance for married persons whose main activity is that of looking after one or more dependent persons (i.e. children under 19 years and elderly or disabled persons). Intended as a support to those married families where one partner is caring, the maximum amount of the allowance in the year of its introduction was €3,809.

As mentioned in Chapter 1, child tax allowances were abolished in 1986. They have not since been re-introduced but tax exemptions for children in low-income families, which were introduced in 1989, have been modestly raised in the intervening period.

3.1.4 Reconciling Work and Family Life

Two social protection measures were taken in the last decade to make it easier for women and/or men to reconcile work and family. In 1997 the regulations were changed whereby time spent looking after children up to twelve years of age, or providing full-time care to a relative in the home, were no longer counted against one when calculating eligibility for pensions. Effectively, a person now has their pension rights frozen, without any adverse effects, while in this situation. This change removes provisions which formerly acted as a penalty on caring and is a measure designed above all to improve the position of women in the home. The Department of Social, Community and Family Affairs has estimated that up to a quarter of a million people, mainly women, are affected by it. The second set of measures related to maternity benefit. The early 1990s saw some significant change in the organisation of maternity benefit. In 1992, the two maternity allowance schemes were rationalised into one payment. The resulting scheme is designed for women who are either in employment immediately before maternity leave (and have the requisite number of contributions) or have the requisite number of contributions during the relevant tax year. Set at €76 in 1992, the minimum value of maternity benefit was raised during the subsequent period to reach €125.3 in 2001. Eligibility for the benefit was extended to part-time workers in 1991 and to the self-employed in 1997. From April 2001, paid maternity benefit was extended in duration by four weeks, bringing its overall duration to eighteen weeks. The period of unpaid maternity leave was also extended, doubled from its prior level to eight weeks. These changes are grounded in a rationale of improving maternity protection legislation as a key component in the development of equality for women.

There is no paid parental leave available in Ireland as of yet. However unpaid parental leave became law in December 1998, granting a statutory entitlement to women and men to avail of a total of 14 weeks of unpaid leave from employment for children born or adopted after May 1998. The leave, which must be taken before the child reaches five years of age, can be taken in a block or on an interspersed basis over a period of time. To qualify the parent must have at least one year's continuous service with the employer. The legislation also allows for *force majeure* leave (paid leave to enable employees to deal with family emergencies resulting from injury or illness of a family member). The maximum duration of this leave is three days in any consecutive 12- month period or five days in any consecutive 36-month period.

In this context it may be relevant also to mention the term-time scheme, although it is not a social security measure. Introduced in December 2000, the term-time initiative was initially a pilot scheme (for three years) to allow working parents to take special unpaid leave around the time when their children have holidays from school. The leave is limited in duration to thirteen weeks and the scheme applies only to civil servants. The leave is also available to civil servants who have care responsibilities for someone in need of care (other than a child) and who lives with them.

3.1.5 Childcare

Only in the mid- to late-1990s did childcare become an issue on the policy agenda in Ireland. It is quite likely that the care of children, which was for long treated as a private matter, has been propelled onto the policy agenda not by gender equality considerations but rather by pressures around labour shortages and economic developments which render the male breadwinner model either outmoded or unfeasible for families. In a national context, where only 17 per cent of all children between the ages of 0 and 9 years are in receipt of paid childcare, the policy scene has been relatively busy of late. Much of this has been what one might call 'pre-policy making activity'.

An Expert Working Group on Childcare was set up in 1997 under the then-prevailing national agreement – Partnership 2000 – with the objective of devising a national framework for the development of childcare services in Ireland. Its report, *National Childcare Strategy,* was published in 1999. In response, the government almost immediately set up an Interdepartmental Committee on Childcare to consider and cost the various proposals in this and other relevant reports. The committee made its recommendations to the government in September 1999. From that date on, the government has made a number of commitments regarding the development of a childcare policy.

With the 'problem' of childcare constructed as a matter of both supply and demand, governmental strategy proposes to address both sides.[15] Among the supply measures, a series of financial incentives (in the form of tax reliefs, tax allowances and capital grants) have been put in place to encourage the private sector (either employers, the voluntary sector or enterprising firms and individuals) to increase the available provision. The National Development Plan 2000 - 2006 provides for an allocation of €317 million to the Department of Justice, Equality and Law Reform to fund the development of childcare services through capital and staffing grant schemes for community-based/non-profit childcare providers. In addition to the €317 million provided under the National Development Plan, the government has made an extra €50.7 million available for the development of childcare. This package is being used to support the development of new areas of the childcare sector and to address several gaps in existing schemes. Measures include start-up grants and other supports for childminders, capital grants for commercial providers and improved grants for community-based childcare projects. In the 2001 budget, some €132 million out of the total provision of €368 million for the period 2000-2006 was allocated to a number of different departments with responsibility for childcare.[16] Among other things, this is to be spent on capital grants for commercial and community-based childcare, the creation of a national after-school initiative and childcare employment grants.

The demand side is more problematic since policy makers have to tread a fine line between providing for those who wish to purchase childcare and not undermining those parents who wish to care for their children themselves. The sensitivity of this issue was referred to by the Minister for Finance in his 1999 budget speech when he warned that consideration would have to be given to the 'question of equity between parents who stay at home to care for children and those who have to meet additional childcare expenses when they go out to work'. No final decisions have yet been made with respect to policies aimed at supporting the general demand for childcare, despite the fact that in the Programme for Prosperity and Fairness the government made a commitment to adopt, before the end of 2000, 'an equitable strategy to support parents in meeting their childcare needs'. The main recommendation of the Expert Working Group on Childcare in this regard was the establishment of a system of tax allowances and subsidies, including personal income tax relief. The option of using child benefit to support childcare was also considered by the Expert Working Group, which noted that this approach had the advantage of being available to all families and of offering women a 'genuine' choice. However, this option was rejected by the group as expensive, since it would require a significant increase in the value of the benefit if it were to have a noticable impact. Despite this recommendation, it is clear that an increased child benefit is the policy measure preferred by government.

Taking an overview, one could identify the following as the objectives of government policy in relation to childcare:

- promote equal opportunities in employment;
- enhance child development;
- combat poverty and social exclusion;
- support family life.

3.1.6 Provisions for the Care of Elderly and Other Adults

3.1.6.1 Benefits for Carers

Ireland was an innovator in this field, recognising very early on (in terms of its own development and before any other European welfare state) that the social welfare system may need to offer support to elderly people in need of care. Hence from 1968, it paid an additional allowance – known as 'prescribed relative's allowance' – to old age and invalidity pension recipients who were receiving full-time care assistance in their own homes from a relative who resided with them. Representing a very different approach, a new benefit for carers was introduced in 1990. The introduction of the means-tested Carer's Allowance in 1990 was a change of policy in a number of respects. First, it represented a switch in terms of which 'arm' of the caring relationship policy to directly support: substituting a payment to the care giver for the existing one to the recipient of care. Secondly, the allowance spelled a broadening of the official view of 'informal supportable' care, on both the receiver and giver ends. In regard to the former, a broader range of benefit recipients qualified as cared-for persons and with regard to the latter the range of eligible carers was broadened to include all married persons. Thirdly, the value of the payment was significantly raised. Recent improvements should be seen as part of a long-standing attempt to raise the status and value of the Carer's Allowance.

Almost from the day of its introduction, this cash benefit has seen continuous expansion and revision. The changes are very numerous as can be seen from Table 3. The main thrust of developments has been three-fold: to make the Carer's Allowance more generous, to gradually extend it to other carers apart from those of the elderly, and to fully integrate the allowance into the social security system (mainly by making recipients eligible for other benefits). As Table 3 shows, practically every aspect of the allowance has been changed. Eligibility has been widened to include carers of ill children and those of ill adults between the ages of sixteen and sixty-five years; some of the conditions, like those of co-residency and non-employment, have been relaxed; some carers were made eligible to receive in-kind benefits; eligibility for other social protection payments has been granted as have credits for social insurance purposes. One of the most important developments in this area of policy in the last years – an indication perhaps that cash benefits for carers have reached their age of majority in the Irish social welfare system – was the introduction in 2000 of a new social insurance-based Carer's Benefit. This is designed to facilitate short-term exit from the work force for the purposes of caring. It is payable for no longer than sixty-five weeks, during which time full employment protection rights apply. In 2001, a carer's leave scheme came into operation, designed to be administered in tandem with the Carer's Benefit. This scheme entitles employees to avail of temporary leave from employment to provide full-time care and attention for a maximum period of sixty five weeks.

An official review of the Carer's Allowance was initiated and reported on in 1998 (Department of Social, Community and Family Affairs, 1998). This had two aims: to assess the purpose and future direction of the allowance and to evaluate expenditure on and the achievements of the programme. Among the issues raised by the review were the need for a multi-disciplinary assessment of a person's care needs for all social and health services, the need for a new continual care payment and the idea of a carer's benefit that would facilitate people in employment to temporarily leave work. These issues will be discussed below in Chapter 6.

Table 3:   *Main Developments in Benefits for Carers of Elderly and Other Adults 1990-2001*

YEAR	MAIN DEVELOPMENTS
1990	Introduction of Carer's Allowance
1991	Coverage extended to persons in receipt of Disabled Person's Maintenance Allowance or EC Bilateral Agreement pensions
1994	• Income disregard of €127 in respect of a spouse's income from employment • Initial income disregard of €2.5 increased to €7.6 • Homemaker's disregard arrangements, preserving carers' entitlement for contributory pension, introduced. Under the new scheme, contribution years spent caring for a child up to 6 years or a frail adult are disregarded in calculating a person's yearly average number of contributions for Old Age Contributory Pension purposes. Up to 20 contribution years may be disregarded
1995	• The age limit for children cared for to qualify for homemakers' disregard increased from 6 to 12 years • Income disregard increased to €190.4 in respect to spouse's income from all sources • Category of persons being cared for extended to include all persons aged 66 or over, regardless of their source of income (previously confined to carers providing care to people aged 66 or over and in receipt of social welfare payments) • Free Travel Companion Pass issued to all care recipients
1996	• Carers receiving Rent or Mortgage Interest Supplements benefit by up to €36.8 a week • Review of Carer's Allowance announced
1997	• Full-time care requirement relaxed to allow care recipients to attend a non-residential course of rehabilitation training or a daycare centre approved by the Minister for Health and Children • an additional 50% paid to persons caring for more than one incapacitated person
1998	• Foreign social security disability pensions up to the maximum of Old Age Contributory Pension not to be assessed as means for Carer's Allowance • Six weeks payment of Carer's Allowance to be paid after the death of a spouse/partner being cared for, who is not getting a social welfare payment • Free Travel Pass for carers getting Carer's Allowance, allowing carers to travel (free) on their own • Review of the Carer's Allowance launched in October

Table 3: **Main Developments in Benefits for Carers of Elderly and Other Adults 1990-2001 (Continued)**

YEAR	MAIN DEVELOPMENTS
1999	• Once-a-year payment of €254 automatically paid to all carers to be used for respite care • All carers providing full-time care and attention to someone over 16 will be eligible to apply for CA regardless income source of care recipient • Full-time carers of children getting domiciliary care (for children between the ages of 2 and 16, severely physically or mentally disabled) entitled to apply for Carer's Allowance • Carers allowed to work part-time for up to 10 h. and still qualify for the allowance. A carer could earn up to €95 a week and still qualify • Condition residency relaxed; carers living "next door" to qualify for Carer's Allowance
1999	• €190.4 income disregard currently applied to a spouse's income to be applied to a couple's joint income. €95.2 weekly disregard to be applied to a single person's income • Social insurance record preserved for persons moving from insurable employment to Carer's Allowance. To date credits have been awarded on an administrative basis. In addition, credits will be awarded when a person with a gap of two years in their paid or credited contributions was in receipt of homemaker disregards before claiming the allowance • Free telephone rental, free travel pass for allowance recipients • Introduction of Home Carer's Tax Allowance • Tax allowance for employing a carer available for relatives other than spouse • Extension of Back to Work Allowance to former carers • €38,092 grant to the Carer's Association towards the cost of producing and distributing an information pack for carers and their families • Extension of the Employment of a Carer Tax Allowance
2000	• New social insurance Carer's Benefit, payable for up to 12 months at €112.3 a week • Annual respite grant increased to €381 • Free electricity allowance and free TV licence extended to recipients of the Carer's Allowance • Carers made eligible for Back to Education Allowance when caring responsibilities have ceased • Carers no longer to satisfy '13 paid contribution' rule when claiming Disability Benefit
2001	• Carer's Allowance increased by €12.6 for carers aged 66 years and over and €10 for those aged under 66 • Annual respite care grant increased by €127 (to €507.8) • Income disregards for means tests for Carer's Allowance relaxed by €63.4 for a single person and €127 for a couple per week

3.1.6.2 Care Services for Ill, Elderly and Disabled Adults

The main provider of care services for frail elderly people in Ireland is the family. For every one elderly person in institutional care, it has been estimated that there are some 3.5 being cared for at home by family members (O'Shea et al, 1991, p. 8). A study by Fahey and Murray (1994) showed that some 21 per cent of the elderly population were receiving substantial informal care of some kind. Moreover, the role of informal family care remains significant even for elderly persons who are heavily dependent. As seen in the last section, support for informal carers has undergone significant development during the 1990s, indicating an increasing recognition, on the part of the state, of their role in Irish society.

Apart from informal care provided by family members, provision of care for elderly, frail and disabled adults is of three types: public, private (predominantly individually-owned nursing homes) and voluntary (predominantly Catholic religious orders operating a not-for-profit service). Over the past decade, trends in the provision of care provided by each sector show a dramatic increase in private provision, while public and voluntary provision has remained more or less stable.

Traditionally, the public sector has been the main provider of institutional care services for the elderly. However, by 1996 the private and voluntary sectors had taken the lead, providing care to 51 per cent of the total of population in extended care facilities during that year (Department of Health and Children, 2000, p. 195).[17] This rapid growth in private provision was brought about by new legislation introduced in 1990 – Health (Nursing Homes) Act 1990 – which set out a new system of state subvention for private nursing home care. Since then, the private nursing sector has enjoyed a period of rapid growth, with close to 6,000 beds available in 1994 compared to 3,272 beds in 1988 (Daly, 1998, p. 31).

However, the new system of subsidies introduced by the 1990 Act has been controversial. To begin with, entitlement is subject to a means test by which the income and assets of the elderly person and his or her spouse are assessed, as well as the income of sons and daughters living in Ireland. Close family are therefore expected to contribute towards the cost of care. However, the legality of this measure is in question since there is no legal or constitutional obligation on family members to support their aged parents in Ireland (Fahey, 1997, pp. 97-98). Secondly, the new legislation has been criticised insofar as, in implementing it, state expenditure on care services for the elderly has been biased towards the private sector while the level of resources available to community care services has been kept low.[18] According to the National Council on Ageing and Older People, this raises serious questions about the financial commitment to maintaining and supporting older people in their homes (Ruddle et al, 1997).

3.1.7 Family Support Services

As the analysis in Chapter 1 has shown, the main orientation of Irish social policy in relation to the family has been to provide cash transfers rather than services. There is evidence, however, that services to families are assuming a greater place on the national agenda. In fact the closing five years of the 1990s witnessed an accelerated move towards public funding of services to families.

Changes made to the structure of the Department of Social, Community and Family Affairs give expression to an increased interest in services for families. The department, having been expanded in 1997 to take on new responsibilities for family policy and services, has undertaken new or expanded funding for community-based, family-related services such as resource centres, counselling and mediation services, as recommended by the Commission on the Family. A new Family Affairs Unit was set up in 1998 within the department with the functions of co-ordinating family policy, pursuing the recommendations of the Commission on the Family which reported in 1998, including funding services, undertaking research and promoting awareness about family issues. This represents a significant new development of and for the department which has tended in the past to have had a classic social protection brief. In 2001 the department's investment in family services amounted to €21 million, compared with just €1.9 million in 1997.

Initiatives are also underway to remove the family support functions of the Department of Social, Community and Family Affairs to a specialist family support agency. A Bill published in 2001 will establish a new statutory body: the Family Support Agency. The new agency will bring together the management and co-ordination of the main programmes and pro-family services developed since 1997. A key objective of the move to create a designated agency for family services is to develop a strong regional network of accessible counselling services for families. In addition to raising awareness about family and parenting issues, it will also undertake research on matters pertaining to family wellbeing.

Family support services are targeted at different types of family need but they all generally involve some form of counselling or advice. They include marriage, child and bereavement counselling services, family mediation services, family and community resource centres and information services. The development of such services was a recommendation of the Commission on the Family.

Family mediation is a state-run service given free of charge to couples in the process of marital breakdown. This service has the aim of ensuring that couples who have decided to separate can easily and speedily access professional assistance. The service provides a forum wherein couples can conduct negotiations concerning residence, finances and parenting in a non-adversarial way. One of the aims of the service is to facilitate an ongoing parenting relationship between a child and both of his/her parents where this is deemed to be in the child's best interest. Since the Family Affairs Unit was set up in 1998, the family mediation service has been established as a nation-wide service, with eleven centres in different locations.[19] Funding has increased from €380,900 in 1997 to €1.7 million in 2001. In 1997, there were only two centres offering this service, one in Dublin – established on a pilot basis in 1986 – and another in Limerick, which opened in 1996. There is a particular background to the expansion of these services. Following the Judicial Separation and Family Law Reform Act 1989, the Family Law (Divorce) Act 1996 and the Children Act 1997, all legal advisers are required to advise clients about reconciliation, mediation and separation agreements in advance of commencing litigation. But the scarcity of places represented a problem for people, especially those living outside Dublin or Limerick.

A second type of family service is that provided by family resource centres. These are local community initiatives, run by either voluntary or community organisations, which receive the bulk if not all of their funding from public sources. These centres provide services for families considered to be in need of extra support (lone parents, young mothers, young fathers, and so forth). Their chief aim is to combat disadvantage and social exclusion by improving the functioning of the family unit. Services provided seek to focus on local neighbourhood solidarity and support as well as mutual care and self-help initiatives. Expansion of the family resource centres has been extremely rapid. They came into being in 1994 when an allocation of €317,435 was made available to the Department of Social Welfare to fund a number of family centres on a three-year pilot basis. In its pre-budget submission of October 1997, the Commission on the Family recommended a significant expansion of the funding available so as to support the establishment of a network of one hundred centres throughout the country. In the 1998 budget, €888,800 was made available to allow for the setting up of between twenty and twenty-five new centres. In the 1999 budget this figure was raised to around €1.2 million which was to facilitate the setting up of twenty extra centres. In the 2001 budget, €5 million was made available for the Family and Community Resource Centre Programme, most of which was committed to existing projects. By the end of 2001 the number of family and community resource centres around the country had risen to eighty.

The third type of service available to families is the marriage, child and bereavement counselling service. The department funds marriage, child and bereavement counselling services by way of once-off grants to organisations providing: marriage counselling services helping people to deal with difficulties which they are experiencing in their relationships; counselling services to children whose lives have been affected by parental separation; and counselling services to bereaved family members. The funding made available by the state has risen from €1.1 million in 1997 to €6 million in 2001.

The aim of marriage counselling is to strengthen family relationships and prevent the break-up of family units. The principal service providers, the Marriage and Relationship Counselling Services and ACCORD, are run by voluntary organisations. Both of these date from the 1960s when they were set up as church initiatives. The former were established in the early 1960s and until 1977 were affiliated to the Church of Ireland. ACCORD, formerly called the Catholic Marriage Advisory Council, was set up in 1968 and became independent in 1975. Up to 1994, grants were channelled to these services through the health boards. In 1994, the Department of Justice, Equality and Law Reform assumed responsibility which in 1998 was transferred to the Department of Social, Community and Family Affairs.

Another type of service for families currently being pioneered is the Family Services Project. The aim is to provide integrated access to information and services for at-risk families in their local area. The development of a one-stop shop concept is integral to the project which has the overall goal of improving the personal circumstances of individuals and families. The philosophy of the project is based on the recognition that community involvement and a local presence are key to successfully delivering support to families. An inter-agency approach is emphasised, involving close working between a range of government organisations and voluntary agencies. A personalised programme of support is made available to a small group of families with complex needs. Introduced in 2000 in three areas – Waterford, Cork and Finglas in Dublin – the government has provided €15.2 million in the National Development Plan for the development of the successful aspects of the project over the period 2000-2006. It is planned to extend the successful elements of the pilot programme in the coming years.

3.1.8 Children's Rights

The late 1990s saw the emergence of children as a target group for social policy, thereby challenging the tendency to locate children within the context of family and to conceive of their welfare in terms of resourcing parents. The National Children's Strategy, published in November 2000, is a major development in Irish social policy. It is highly innovative in a number of respects. In the first instance, it is a statement to and about children – hence it could be said to be akin to a 'children's policy'. In the second instance, it recognises children as individuals and to some extent treats them as a group with interests that need to be reflected in the public policy agenda. Thirdly, it grants children rights. Based on what is called a coherent and inclusive view of childhood, a three-fold strategy is laid out to:

• give children a voice by enhancing their opportunities for participation in and influence on matters affecting them;
• improve understanding of childhood in Ireland through research, evaluation and information on children's rights, needs and the effectiveness of services;
• offer children and their families better services and supports which are more focused on their needs, encompass a full range of needs and address an agenda of equity and inclusiveness.

Some of the proposals are very far-reaching even in an international context. In line with the 'voice' proposal for example, a National Children's Parliament has been set up and has already met, bringing together 250 children aged between seven and seventeen years. This is intended to be a forum wherein children can raise and debate on a periodic basis issues of concern to them. This is to be complemented by activities to enhance the representation of children's interests at other levels of decision making. Following practice elsewhere in Europe,[20] an Ombudsman for Children, designed to promote the rights and welfare of children and to examine and investigate complaints, is also to be established. At governmental level a Children's Advisory Council has been set up and has been given the task of advising the Minister for Children on all aspects of policy relating to children's lives. As well as institutionalising the representation of their interests, the strategy is also strong on service provision. Locality-based services are emphasised as is the degree of coherence and integration among services in different domains. The range of services, especially those which provide opportunities for developmental, play, cultural and leisure activities, is to be improved as is the availability of childcare and early educational initiatives and health services. The needs of children living in disadvantaged situations are also prioritised for attention. A central part of the strategy is to protect or improve the quality of children's family life. In policy terms this is translated into measures such as parenting education and support as well as services targeted on disadvantaged families. The advantages of this strategy are not only that it sets out a detailed policy but that it provides an elaborated policy framework.

Overall, the National Children's Strategy is in our view a very large development in Irish public policy. It initiates a broad-based series of measures to recognise and create children as social citizens.

3.2 The Objectives of Family Policy Reform in Ireland in the 1990s

Two development trajectories were to be seen in family policy in Ireland in the 1990s. One might be characterised as 'consolidation', the other as 'transformation'. Both are significant. The measures described as consolidation include those focused on existing programmes. They consist mainly of prioritising child benefits for development, increasing generosity and scope of benefits for carers and the consolidation of several benefits for women and men rearing children on their own into the One-Parent Family Payment. Note that in making child benefit so generous, policy makers may actually be changing its intent – from a payment designed to help families with the costs of children to a payment for the care of children.

The second line of development of family policy is here labelled as 'transformative'. One of the hallmarks of this trajectory is that policy has taken a broader remit, focusing on target groups and innovative measures rather than existing policy programmes. What this has meant in practice is that the debate has a much larger canvas than existing policy approaches. So the Commission on the Family chose to approach its task by first setting out principles and proceeding from these to a consideration of policy and policy reform. The main transformative currents are the Commission on the Family (set up in 1995 and reporting in 1998), the National Childcare Strategy in 1999 and the National Children's Strategy which was produced in November 2000.

One clear objective of policy in the 1990s was to raise the level of income support given to families with children. Judging from the measures taken in recent years, the government appears to have decided to achieve this through a general set of increases rather than more targeted measures. However, opinion differs on the most appropriate goal and means of child income support. A second tendency has been to prioritise children. This is in some sense part of a trend for policy to direct its attention to intra-familial matters but it also represents a significant interest on the part of policy in children in their own right. Policy appears to be heading in the direction of granting children some rights as citizens. This would be very radical in an Irish context where the social rights of adults in Ireland have seldom been framed in a discourse of citizenship. That is, with means-tested benefits forming such a large tranche of cash transfers in the Irish case, the development of the Irish welfare state was for long about meeting need rather than granting a generous set of benefits to which people are entitled as of right.

Care has come into its own, having been a major concern of Irish family policy in the 1990s. Care for the elderly as well as that for children have received attention, but whereas childcare only entered the policy agenda in the late 1990s, care of elderly and ill adults was a focus of policy throughout the decade. Looking at the treatment of care by the social protection arrangements in Ireland, it is interesting to observe significant differences in the way the state is responding to the care of children and that of the elderly. The latter is a policy of expansion – one of enticing people to care for elderly or ill adults by offering them an increasingly more generous payment for this purpose. The rhetoric around the expansion of benefits for carers of elderly and ill adults tends to be grounded in a discourse about giving official recognition to the role of carer. Developments around the elderly should therefore be interpreted mainly in terms of a greater need for home-based care at a time when the supply of private care is diminishing (because of greater female employment). The contrast with policy on the care of children is very striking. This is treated with great caution and it is unlikely that the social protection sector will play a significant role in changing existing, largely informal, provision. Amidst a clamour for childcare services, the government has found it increasingly difficult to negotiate the terrain between the rights and responsibilities of parents in different situations. At present there is much pressure on the government for action on childcare. The response thus far has been very particular. Although a lot of money has been devoted to encouraging the development of a childcare sector, Irish social policy remains within a traditional mould. This is especially the case in that the state is not involved to any significant degree in service provision. It is, rather, a funder and a facilitator of private, market or community sector services.

In relation to lone parents, one could characterise reforms in the 1990s as recognising them as a sector of the population with legitimate welfare needs. While provision for different groups of lone mothers had been in existence since the 1970s, the integration of the different measures into a single scheme in 1990 and its extension to male lone parents consolidated provision. A second tendency was to broaden the conception of lone parents to include a notion of (and the possibility of becoming a) worker. At the present time, policy for lone parents seeks to encourage them to consider employment as an alternative to long-term welfare receipt while at the same time supporting them to remain full-time in the home if that is their wish. This is a rather difficult balance to maintain. In general, benefit provision could be said to favour the model of a stay-at-home mother since it has no elements to compel the lone parent (most of whom are women) into employment. The absence of any time limits – lone parents can receive the payment until a child is twenty-two years of age – is especially significant in this respect.[21]

The next chapter moves on to consider how family-related policy developed in the UK, Sweden, France and Germany in the course of the 1990s.

Chapter 4

Reform in Other European Countries and How Ireland Compares

As mentioned already, Ireland is different to most of its European neighbours in that planning and decision making for much of the 1990s was taking place in a climate of financial surplus and general consensus about the need to improve both social protection and the situation of low-income families (especially those in employment). It is important not to make too much of these differences though, for it is not clear that they are all that relevant to family policy. In other words, it may be that, compared with other domains of social policy, decisions about family policy are influenced in a different way or to a differential degree by financial matters. Given that family policy is under-studied, especially from a comparative perspective, researchers are not yet in a position to be definitive about how it is affected by the state of the economy (Kaufmann, 1990, 1993).

Context aside, family policy is a very active arena of policy in each of the four European countries chosen for comparison with Ireland in this report. Since the purpose of this chapter is to compare developments across a range of countries so that we can better understand policy responses in Ireland and elsewhere, the discussion to follow will be organised along similar lines as the last chapter. Hence, it will treat of measures for children, lone parents, and so forth in turn. The concentration is on reforms in the last ten years. Description (as against analysis) of provision will be limited to where it is considered essential. The latest available information at the time of writing is used throughout; most often this refers to mid-2001 (most often July). For ease of understanding, the four countries will be considered in the same sequence under each heading. We begin with the UK (on the grounds that its model most closely resembles the Irish case), then proceed to Sweden, France and Germany.

4.1 Changes in Cash Benefits for Families with Children

4.1.1 Child Benefit

4.1.1.1 Child Benefit in the UK

Child benefit in the UK is, as in Ireland, the only universal benefit and its primary purpose is to meet the costs associated with bringing up children. The benefit is non-taxable, non-contributory and non-income related. It is paid for all children aged under sixteen years (or nineteen for those who remain in full-time education).[22] Paid normally to the mother, it has tended to be more generous than its Irish equivalent. The rates for the year 2001 are £10.35 (€16.9) per child per week; although there are higher rates for the eldest child – £15.50 (€25.3) for a two-parent and £17.55 (€28.6) for a lone-parent family.[23] In a further difference to Ireland, child benefit counts as income for recipients of means-tested benefits, the value of which is reduced pound for pound by child benefit. Although child benefit has been the subject of public controversy in recent years, embroiled in a debate about whether it should or should not be taxed, the last three governments have been committed to preserving its universality. Its development over the decade has however been sporadic. In 1991 the benefit was increased, having been frozen between 1987 and 1991, and from 1992 on its value was indexed in line with prices. In 1999, the New Labour government in a major policy development increased the value of child benefit by 20 per cent over and above inflation.[24]

4.1.1.2 Child Benefit in Sweden

In Sweden child benefit is non-taxable and paid to all parents for each child under sixteen years or, if the child remains in education, until he or she leaves compulsory school. Families with three or more children are entitled to a 'large family supplement'. The benefit saw little change over the course of the 1990s. Entitlement was unchanged and payment rates remained more or less stable over the decade. However, there was a dip in the mid years of the decade, coinciding with a general period of welfare cut-backs in Sweden. Thus, between 1996 and 1998 the value of the child benefit was reduced by 15 per cent and the large family supplement was abolished. In 1998, however, child benefit rates were increased to their 1995 levels and the large family supplement was restored. In 2000 and 2001 the benefit was increased in value, by 13 per cent and 12 per cent respectively.

4.1.1.3 Child Benefit in France

In France the principal cash benefit programme for families with children is the family allowance – *Allocations Familiales*. This benefit is not totally comparable to child benefit since it is a payment made to and intended for the family as a whole.[25] The benefit is non-taxable and payable to all families with children from the birth of the second child until the children reach the age of nineteen years (twenty for children in education or training or when unemployed). The value of the benefit increases with both the number and age of children. Families with three or more children may be entitled to a 'large family supplement'. This supplement is income-related, although around 80 per cent of large families secure entitlement to it.

France has seen a lot of change in relation to cash payments for families with children. During the past decade, the pillars of French family policy have been the subject of much public debate and controversy. The principal alteration to the universal family allowance programme was to make it subject to a means-test in 1998. This measure was taken by the socialist Jospin government but it drew on reforms suggested by the previous government in the ill-fated *Plan*

Juppé. Plans for a reform in family policy began in 1995, as part of a broader plan of social security reform *(Plan Juppé).* This plan was drawn up in an attempt to reduce a serious budget deficit in the social security system and included reforms in family policy.[26] In order to achieve objectives like equity and bringing 'balance' back to the family policy budget, the plan included measures to freeze the value of benefits and increase the extent of means-testing and tax liability in relation to family benefits. *Plan Juppé* was never fully implemented though. The Jospin government, which came to power in 1997, revisited some of the issues which led to *Plan Juppé*, especially that of equity. The new government's general view was that the principle of equity involves excluding rich families from family allowances and targeting low-income and poor families. In other words, equity is to be understood as the vertical redistribution of wealth from the rich to the poor. Opponents of Jospin's reform invoked a very different conception of equity and questioned which type of equity is most appropriate to French family policy. The family associations (which in France are well-organised and have quite a strong foothold in the policy-making process) argued that, although family policy is a powerful instrument in the fight against poverty, it should not be confused with it. Invoking a classic understanding of family policy, they held that the conception of equity as vertical redistribution from the rich to the poor (the business of social policy in general) should be distinguished from equity, understood as horizontal redistribution from celibates to families (the concern of family policy proper). Apart from the family associations, other opponents of the selectivity proposal defended the universality principle on different grounds, for example as a republican ideal (Bouget, 1998). With such opposition, Jospin's measure to target family allowances lasted only a few months.[27] Several months later, the measure was rescinded and the universality of the benefit restored.

4.1.1.4 Child Benefit in Germany

In Germany a very significant change in child benefit (*Kindergeld*) took place in 1996 when the family allowances were restructured. The reform was occasioned by a decision of the Federal Constitutional Court, which found that some existing tax and cash transfer measures were detrimental to the position of the family as stated in the constitution (Bahle and Rothenbacher, 1996, p.25). Prior to that year, family allowances consisted of a dual system of tax allowances and cash benefits whereby it was possible for both to be claimed by a family. Thus, all parents of children up to the age of sixteen years[28] were entitled to a child benefit which varied according to family income and number of children. In addition, all parents in employment were entitled to a child tax allowance and those who did not make full use of it received a supplement to child benefit. With the reform of 1996, the possibility of dual entitlement to both child benefit and child tax allowance was abolished and an option introduced to choose between them (except for claimants outside the tax net who can claim only child benefit). At the same time, the reduction in the value of child benefit for families with higher incomes was abolished, as was the supplement to child benefit for families with low incomes,[29] while the value of both the child benefit and child tax allowance were significantly increased – a measure which benefited especially low to average income families. In addition, the general age threshold was increased from sixteen to eighteen years. Another change associated with the reform was for child benefit to be in most cases paid out directly through the wage-slip as a tax credit.[30] This practice is not followed for claimants who are not in employment and those working in a firm with fewer than fifty employees; in those cases it is paid directly by the Family Fund (*Familienkasse*).

Since the 1996 reform, the value of both child benefit and child tax allowance has been increased several times. For example, between 1992 and 2001, the value of the child benefit for the first child almost quadrupled, increasing from €35.7 to €138 a month, while the value of the benefit for the third child increased by 36 per cent.

Table 4 shows the value of child benefits in mid-2001 across the different countries (presented in euro for ease of comparison). It shows that there is a lot of variation in how countries configure their cash supports for families with children, mainly in regard to the value of the payments made to families as the number of children rises. Germany pays the most generous child benefits for all family sizes. Sweden is the second most generous country in this regard. While its relative position is now much more favourable than it was, Ireland still lags somewhat behind the continental European countries and Sweden, although not the UK when it comes to larger families. However, it is important to remember that, in terms of the overall level of support to families with children, Ireland would still be in a laggard position because most of these countries also direct significant support for families with children through the taxation system (whereas this is only minimal in Ireland).

Table 4: *Child Benefits in Ireland, UK, Sweden, France and Germany (monthly rates €, July 2001)*

	Ireland	UK[a]	Sweden	France	Germany
1 child	85.7	108.2	105.4	-	138
2 children	171.4	180.5	220	108.8	277.1
3 children	280.6	252.8	355.74[b]	390[c]	430.5

a Since child benefit is paid weekly in the UK, amounts have been calculated based on a 30-day month.

b Supplements for large families are included in this figure.

c Supplements for large families are included in this figure since they are received by around 80 per cent of families with three or more children. The supplement is paid to families with annual earnings up to €30,025 (dual-earner couples and lone-parent families) or €25,545 (one-earner couples).

4.1.2 In-work Benefits

Since the UK is the only country of the four to have an in-work benefit (like Ireland), the discussion here will be limited to developments there. This approach to income support has been a major focus of policy attention in the UK for at least ten years now. Almost irrespective of whether the Conservatives or Labour held power, reform undertaken in the UK has sought to make cash benefits less generous and employment more attractive. Sometimes quite drastic measures have been taken. The reforms have certainly been diverse. As in Ireland, consistent improvements have been made to the in-work benefit – Family Credit – to make it more generous. In 1992 the hours threshold for qualification for Family Credit was lowered from twenty-four to sixteeen hours a week. In 1994 a childcare disregard was introduced for Family Credit recipients for the first time. However, the most important development was the replacement, in 2000, of Family Credit by a new Working Families' Tax Credit. This is a benefit with broadly the same entitlement rules as those of Family Credit but it is paid through tax rather than social security. As well as transferring key aspects of income support from social security to tax, the move to the Working Families' Tax Credit has led to a new Childcare Tax Credit[31] and a decrease in the benefit taper. One important feature of this reform is that it especially targets the employment of lone mothers, not only by introducing more generous help towards the costs of childcare but also through a total child maintenance disregard.[32]

4.1.3 Family-related Taxation

4.1.3.1 Taxation in the UK

The UK is the leading innovator here also. A new Children's Tax Credit was introduced in 2001 as part of the general welfare to work policy. This is payable to families with at least one child aged under sixteen years.[33] It works in a similar fashion to the Married Couple's Allowance – a tax credit available for married couples that was abolished in the year 2000. However it is more generous. It consists of an income tax relief up to a set amount (£442 - €720) per family but for those earning over £32,785 (€53,373) the credit is reduced at the rate of £1 (€1.6) for every £15 (€24.4) of income taxed at the higher rate. In the long term, the Children's Tax Credit is expected to be integrated with the allowances for children in Income Support, Job Seeker's Allowance and Working Families' Tax Credit, thus bringing together the different elements of benefits payable for children into a system of support that is envisaged to be seamless (Howard, 1999). This measure is part of New Labour's Welfare to Work strategy, its primary aim being to reduce the barriers to employment.

4.1.3.2 Taxation in Sweden

There were no changes of note in regard to taxation in Sweden over the period.

4.1.3.3 Taxation in France

France operates a system of compulsory joint taxation for couples and their children (*Quotient Familial*).[34] During the past decade, the redistributive role of this family tax scheme was questioned by some family associations, such as the CNAF,[35] and other social partners in the light of the plan to subject child benefits to a means test. The CNAF made the point that the redistributive effects intended by subjecting the benefit to a means test were either decreased, neutralised or reversed by the *Quotient Familial*. This is the case because, given the progressive character of taxation, the system favours wealthy families since the value of the allowances increases with income.[36] Given this, it was announced in 1998 that the income ceiling for eligibility for the tax allowances would be lowered except for lone-parent families. It was estimated that 530,000 families would be affected by this measure, most belonging to the highest decile of disposable income (Gillot, 1998). The measure was made effective for revenue earned in 1999 but it continues to be opposed by some family associations because it disfavours rich families with children in comparison to rich childless people. According to one of these associations, although it is appropriate for the rich to pay higher taxes than the poor, it is not normal that rich families with children should pay higher taxes than rich single persons without children *(Familles de France)*.

4.1.3.4 Taxation in Germany

In Germany the major reform of the family support system involved changes in child tax allowances as well as changes in child benefit. Both types of changes were outlined under 4.1.1.4 above.

4.2 Provision for Lone Parents

4.2.1 Provision for Lone Parents in the UK

The UK appears to be in the process of opting for a mixed role of parent and worker for lone parents. A New Deal for Lone Parents was introduced in 1998, offering help and advice on jobsearch, training, childcare and other employment-related matters. It is designed to help lone parents on Income Support to find a job. It is part of New Labour's Welfare to Work strategy and consists of a mix of subsidies to employers, job-search assistance, training and direct job creation. Unlike new deals for other groups of benefit recipients, the New Deal for Lone Parents is voluntary insofar as the social security system does not require lone parent claimants to be available for work in order to be eligible for benefits. However, other measures operate in the direction of increasing the incentives for lone parents to seek employment.

The main thrust of reform under New Labour (as indeed under their predecessors) is to increase the attractiveness of work. Some measures in line with this general ethos have been especially targeted at lone parents – for example, lone parent premiums in Income Support, Child Benefit and Job Seeker's Allowance were abolished in 1998. Since 1994, lone parents on in-work benefits have received financial assistance towards the costs of childcare in the form of childcare disregards or, more recently, credits, while lone parents on Income Support or Job Seeker's Allowance have no right to this sort of assistance.

Another innovation in the 1990s in the UK was the introduction of a state agency to secure maintenance for parents bringing up children on their own. The Child Support Agency, set up in 1993 by the Conservative government, seeks to ensure that absent fathers contribute to the support of their children. It assesses the levels of maintenance according to a highly complex formula and enforces payment from absent parents by imposing criminal sanctions in the case of failure or refusal to pay. Lone parents claiming Income Support or Job Seeker's Allowance are required to register with the Agency and provide information on the whereabouts of the absent parent. Failure to provide the information required (unless there is good cause for not doing so) is subject to penalties. Should they receive maintenance, they have their benefit reduced pound for pound since any maintenance received counts as income when calculating the amount of the benefit to which they are entitled. The Agency has been both controversial and unpopular. Yet the New Labour government has not only not abolished the Agency but has endorsed the policy underpinning it. It has introduced a series of reforms which are designed to promote compliance and to reduce some of the work disincentives implicit in the current scheme (both for absent parents and parents involved in providing care). These were set out in the Child Support, Pensions and Social Security Act which received Royal Assent in July 2000. The Child Support Agency is to introduce the reforms for new cases from April 2002. The essence of these reforms involves: (a) a simplification of the formula for calculating the amount of child maintenance, (b) a reduction in the level of maintenance required from liable parents on low income or those bringing up children in a second family, (c) stricter penalties for absent parents refusing to pay (e.g. fines for providing false information, disqualification from driving, civil imprisonment), and

(d) 10 per cent disregards for child support for Income Support recipients and full (100 per cent) disregards for those in receipt of tax credits.[37]

4.2.2 Provision for Lone Parents in Sweden

In Sweden lone parents have the right to a minimum guaranteed maintenance payment for each child. This payment may come from the other parent, from the state, or from a combination of both. In 1997 a new system of child support came into operation. The objective was to tighten the rules of the child support system so as to ensure that liable parents fulfilled their obligations. Under the new arrangements, a maintenance allowance is paid by the state if the parent fails to pay, or if the maintenance payment is less than 1,173 SEK (€130) per month. The maintenance allowance is also paid in full in cases where paternity has not been established, when the other parent is deceased or when the child has been adopted by one parent. Liable parents are, however, obliged to reimburse all or part of the advanced maintenance allowance to the state. In cases where a parent has difficulties in making payments, the state provides a number of facilities such as respite and concession loans. Such loans are subject to interest so that the amount of debt increases as it accumulates.

4.2.3 Provision for Lone Parents in France

In France a designated means-tested allowance exists for lone parents (*Allocation de Parent Isolé*). Apart from this, lone parents who are not receiving maintenance payments from the absent parent are entitled, under certain conditions, to a guaranteed maintenance allowance paid by the family fund of the social security (*Allocation de Soutien Familial*).

The guaranteed maintenance allowance is automatically paid to lone parents when the other parent is dead or when paternity has not been established. In cases where the liable parent fails to pay child maintenance, the family fund of the social security is in charge of seeking out the absent parent in order to ensure that payments are made. In the meantime, a maintenance allowance is paid to the lone parent in the form of an advance payment, which must be later reimbursed by the absent parent.

The lone parent's allowance, introduced in 1976, is intended to assist lone parents, overwhelmingly women, with little or no income due either to loss of a prior source of income because of separation or divorce or to an inadequate employment record (e.g. very young single mothers). The allowance was financed by the family fund of social security since its creation until 1999, when the state took charge of its financing in order to allow the family fund to finance the re-establishment of the child benefit as a universal benefit (described under 4.1.1.3 above). Despite the existence of a designated payment for them, however, relatively high numbers of French lone mothers are to be found among the recipients of the minimum income programme (*Revenu Minimum d'Insertion*). This is because the right to the lone-parent's allowance ends when the child reaches the age of three. According to recent data, while there was an increase of 39.8 per cent in the number of lone-parent families between 1982 and 1998, the unemployment rate among these families during the same period grew by some 65.7 per cent (INED, 1999).[38]

The government's response to this situation has been to introduce a series of employment incentives for lone parents. In fact, the most significant changes in policy for lone parents during the 1990s have taken place in this area. Recipients of the lone parent's allowance who are entering paid employment are now entitled to a 100 per cent earnings disregard for a period of up to six months. After that, they obtain a 50 per cent disregard for the following nine months. While in receipt of the allowance, lone parents are also entitled to enrol in vocational training programmes traditionally reserved for the long-term unemployed. Also, for those in charge of very young children (0-3 years old), crèche fees may be significantly reduced.

4.2.4 Provision for Lone Parents in Germany

In Germany, lone parents who are receiving insufficient or no maintenance payments for children from the other parent have the right to an advance on maintenance from the government for children up to the age of twelve years for a maximum of six years. However, in the case of divorced or separated lone parents, their own parents are looked to first for support before the state will pay. Unmarried mothers are exempt from this rule. This has been attributed to the Abortion Law compromise, according to which exemption rules are designed to prevent unmarried women from having an abortion for economic reasons or for fear of becoming dependent on their parents (Ostner, 1997, p. 42). The only real change in the 1990s related to the value of the maintenance payment; between 1994 and 2000 the maximum was decreased from €180 a month to €151 (in the old Länder).

4.3 Reconciling Work and Family

4.3.1 Reconciling Work and Family in the UK

The UK has again seen the most activity in this sphere of policy. There are two main reasons for this. First, the change in government in 1997 heralded a change in receptivity towards EU policies and, secondly, the UK has been a laggard in this aspect of policy and so has considerable catching up to do. The UK resembles Ireland in that reconciliation is a relatively new issue for public policy. Government in the UK has traditionally taken a non-interventionist stance with regard to the family-employment relationship (mainly in the belief that this is a decision best left to the family itself). Policy towards the family has been based on the principle of individual rather than collective responsibility, while labour market policy has imposed minimal regulation in the view that this encourages economic growth. As a result, reconciliation arrangements have been regarded as a private matter for individuals to manage by themselves or in conjunction with their families or employers.

The determination to maintain a minimal level of regulation in the labour market, together with a belief in individual responsibility, led the Conservative governments of the 1980s and 1990s to opt out of the Charter of Fundamental Social Rights of Workers (signed in Strasbourg in 1989) and the Agreement on Social Policy (annexed to the Treaty on the European Union signed in Maastricht in 1992). The grounds were that regulation would impinge on the private lives of individuals and impose a heavy burden on employers. The Charter contained important directives on the family-employment relationship, especially in relation to parental leave and other leaves for family reasons as well as protection for part-time workers against unfair treatment by employers.[39] Until very recently the UK had no statutory parental leave and part-time workers – mainly women – had inferior rights to those working full-time. In addition, the UK was the only member state without a universal right to maternity leave for women in paid employment when the directive on the protection of pregnant women was introduced in 1992. Although the UK opposed the Pregnant Workers Directive initially, it was finally implemented (albeit in a minimalist way) in 1993.[40] Against this background, employers had been encouraged to provide family-friendly arrangements for their employees. Some employers did so, offering part-time working arrangements, workplace nurseries, parental leave (paid or unpaid) and maternity benefits beyond the statutory minimum. The level of provision was uneven, though, with higher quality and a wider range of provision being found in female-dominated workplaces, in the public sector or in large private sector firms (Lewis, 1999).

With the accession of New Labour to power in 1997, the UK's opt-out of the Agreement on Social Policy was reversed. As a result, European directives relevant to the reconciliation of work and family life have been implemented. They include the Working Time Directive (in 1998), the Parental Leave Directive and time-off for caring for dependants (in 1999) and the Part-Time Work Directive (in 2000). However it is important to emphasise that these directives were implemented in a minimalist way, in accordance with long-standing principles governing family and labour policies in the UK and a determination to cut public expenditure. Thus, the new legislation in the UK provides only a set of minimal statutory rights which employers can extend according to their will, needs and circumstances. The government encourages employers to go beyond the statutory minimum (through promotional campaigns offering advice and information to employers about the benefits of family-friendly policies for their business) yet it provides no money to help employers to do so.[41]

Statutory parental leave (for both mothers and fathers) was introduced in the UK in December 1999. This parental leave is unpaid. Each parent is entitled to thirteen weeks in total for each child, which can be taken in short or long blocks (depending on what has been agreed with the employer) up until the child's fifth birthday. Employers and unions are encouraged to reach collective agreements on how to manage parental leave; otherwise a default parental leave scheme set by the government applies. Under the default scheme, parental leave is to be taken in blocks or multiples of one week, up to a maximum of four weeks a year and, where businesses cannot cope, it is subject to postponement by the employer for up to six months (except in cases where parental leave is taken immediately after the child's birth). Employment rights apply during the leave period. In a related development, employees were granted in December 1999 the right to take a 'reasonable' period of time off work to deal with an emergency involving a 'dependant.'[42] There is no set limit to the amount of time that can be taken; it is left to the employer's discretion. Also, the right does not include a statutory right to pay, so whether or not the employee will be paid is at the employer's discretion.

The introduction of parental leave led to further changes in maternity leave and maternity benefits; these changes are significant given the UK's relatively poor maternity provision. In December 1999, the entitlement to maternity leave was extended from fourteen to eighteen weeks so as to align it with the period of entitlement to Statutory Maternity Pay. The employment requirement for extended maternity leave was reduced from two years to one year in order to match it with the qualifying period for parental leave. Changes (applying to women expecting babies on or after 20 August 2000) were also made to the conditions of eligibility for Maternity Allowance and the amounts paid so as to extend the benefit to the lower paid.[43] These changes break the link between employment status and payment levels. Further reforms to maternity provisions were announced in March 2001. These include: (a) a 60 per cent increase in the value of weekly maternity pay, (b) an extension of the period of maternity pay from eighteen to twenty-six weeks alongside an extension to maternity leave and (c) the introduction of two weeks paid paternity leave. These reforms will come into full effect in April 2003.

4.3.2 Reconciling Work and Family in Sweden

Sweden provides a strong contrast to the UK and Ireland. Its policies on reconciling family and work are amongst the most comprehensive in Europe. At present, a wide range of provisions allow workers to take time off work to attend to family responsibilities, such as caring for children and for frail adult relatives. These provisions include paid leave of absence to care for children and adult relatives (both of which can also be taken on a part-time basis) and the possibility of working reduced hours. In Sweden reconciliation policies are firmly targeted on gender equality. They aim to: (a) encourage women to take up paid work, (b) enable women to combine (paid) work with motherhood, and (c) increase equality between women and men in everyday life.

One characteristic of Swedish reconciliation policies is that entitlement rights are closely tied to gainful employment. Hence women are strongly encouraged to take up paid work and build a career before starting a family. However Swedish policies are also informed by important egalitarian and universalist principles. Such principles are clearly reflected in both the basis and unit of entitlement. Although entitlement depends on previous gainful employment, the system also allows unemployed persons to qualify for a minimum guaranteed benefit. Alternative arrangements are in place for people who do not qualify for parental leave benefit at all.[44] The unit of entitlement is normally the individual rather than the family and, in some cases, entitlement rights are non-transferable. This is very important from the point of view of gender equality since it provides an incentive for fathers to take on caring responsibilities.

However, in the mid-1990s Sweden saw its highest levels of unemployment for several decades, occasioned by a serious economic recession. This led some authors to question the impact of the new situation on existing policy and benefit take-up rates (Nasman, 1999). While the economic crisis of the 1990s brought cuts in and lower take-up rates for some benefits,[45] policy development in the area has moved towards increased individualisation of rights and better provision for the care of ill, adult relatives.

At present parental leave in Sweden is available for a total of 450 days, which can be taken at any time until the child is eight years of age. The mother can make use of 60 of these days before childbirth, while the rest can be shared between parents at their discretion.[46] Following moves made in 1995 towards further individualisation, 60 days of the leave were reserved for the mother and father (30 days each) – the so-called 'father/mother month'. During these 30 days, the right to parental leave is individual and non-transferable (except for lone parents and if the second parent does not qualify for parental leave). Since 1995, each parent has the right to a maximum of 180 and a minimum of 30 days of paid leave. These 360 days are paid at an 80 per cent wage replacement rate (and the remaining 90 days at a lower rate). By encouraging fathers to take parental leave, these measures are quite a radical way of promoting gender equality both in the workplace and in the home. At the same time, the government has granted special funds to municipalities, county councils, labour organisations and public insurance offices for a number of information and educational projects on paternity and parental leaves. There is also a temporary paid parental leave to allow parents to care for a sick child. In 1994 this was cut, as part of a general set of retrenchment measures, from 120 to 60 days a year. Further changes to the parental leave scheme were announced in 2001. One of the main objectives of these reforms is to increase the number of fathers taking up parental leave. Changes include: (a) extension of parental leave from 12 to 13 months, (b) extension of the parental leave period earmarked for fathers from one month to two months, and (c) increased flexibility regarding working hours. These changes took effect in January 2002.

4.3.3 Reconciling Work and Family in France

In France reconciling employment and family life is also an important issue for family policy given relatively high levels of female employment. A wide range of policies is in place to affect the way parents can combine their family and work obligations. These include leave regulations and cash benefits, labour legislation concerning part-time work, childcare services and school schedules. According to some analysts, policies related to reconciling family and work in France are geared towards giving women a true choice by supporting them both as mothers and workers (Hantrais and Letablier, 1996). However, during the first half of the 1990s, against a backdrop of growing unemployment, labour market considerations played a decisive role in reconciliation policies, while matters pertaining to equal opportunities were largely ignored (Fagnani, 1998; Jenson and Sineau, 1998). Thus, for example, changes in parental leave schemes were geared towards reducing unemployment rates and freeing up jobs; part-time work legislation was focused on reducing employment costs; and changes in childcare provision sought to create new jobs. However, the more recent reforms signal a change in policy, since they are principally aimed at encouraging fathers to become involved in the care of their children.

With regard to parental leave, the main changes during the 1990s have been directed at extending coverage. Since 1995 for example, no employer, in whatever size of company, can refuse an employee her or his right to unpaid parental leave. In the same year, job protection guarantees were improved.

For example, employees got the right to take up professional training during the leave period. Changes were also made to the parental allowance which was originally introduced in 1985 for parents interrupting their professional activity to raise a third or subsequent child. In 1994 the allowance was extended to families with two children in the name of 'free choice for parents' (Fagnani, 1998). In the same year, measures were taken to target the allowance on economically active mothers. The links with previous employment career were tightened – to be eligible, parents with two children had to have two years of professional activity within the five years preceding the birth of the child.[47] Reforms were also made in order to encourage part-time work as a means of reconciling work and family life. The parental allowance was made available to parents who only partially interrupt their professional activity and was paid according to the duration of their work (previously it was only available if the child was at least two years of age). In addition, it was made possible for both parents to benefit from this option at the same time, although the sum of the benefits received by each was never to be superior to that of the full benefit.[48] In 1994 a three-day unpaid leave for parents looking after a sick child was introduced (five days if the child is under one year or if the employee has three children or more, all under sixteen years).

With regard to maternity and paternity leaves, the most significant change has been the extension of the paid paternity leave scheme from three to fourteen days. Under this new measure, fathers will be entitled to take time off from work for a period of two weeks within the four months following the birth of their child, while retaining 100 per cent of their (net) salary. This measure was announced in June 2001 to take effect in January 2002.

Another reconciliation strategy pursued in France during the 1990s was that of increasing the supply of and demand for part-time employment. New legislation aiming at encouraging part-time employment, directed at both employers and employees, was introduced between 1992 and 1994. One measure taken was to reduce the cost of part-time employment. Since 1992, employers can benefit from a

30 per cent reduction in their social security costs for (permanent) part-time contracts of a certain duration of working hours per week (between eighteen and thirty-two hours). This legislation has been said to work to the benefit of the employer rather than the employee however, producing what can be called 'imposed' rather than 'chosen' part-time work (Descolonges and Fagnani, 1998). This distinction is important because 'imposed' part-time work can be a serious obstacle to reconciling family and work obligations.[49] Because public childcare facilities are open only during normal working hours, reconciling family and work responsibilities for part-time women can be a much more arduous task than for those in full-time employment with more typical schedules. With little reward from work, plus the difficulty of finding affordable childcare that matches their timetables,[50] most women in this sector stop working altogether upon the birth of a second child, thereby qualifying for the full parental leave payment. A second goal of French policy during the 1990s has been to give employees a more genuine choice of part-time work in order to better reconcile family and work. Among the relevant measures here was new legislation giving employees the option to switch from full-time to part-time work and vice versa (in cases where such work is available). Furthermore, a new modality of part-time work contracts was introduced. These are organised on an annual basis to give employees the possibility of taking some time off work during the year for the purposes of attending to family responsibilities (for example, during school holidays).

4.3.4 Reconciling Work and Family in Germany

Germany saw much more policy activity in this area during the 1980s as compared with the 1990s (Lüscher et al, 1990). In the 1980s an 18-month parental leave was introduced together with a parental allowance in the form of a flat-rate payment for a stay-at-home parent caring for young children. Policy activity in the 1990s mainly consisted of minor changes to this set of provisions, apart from reforms passed in the year 2000. In 1992 the period of parental leave was extended from eighteen months to three years and in 1993 the duration of the paid component of the leave was extended from eighteen to twenty-four months. In 1994, access to the parental allowance was delimited when entitlement was made subject to an upper income limit for the first six months after childbirth.[51]

A major reform of the parental leave arrangements was passed by the upper house of the German parliament in July 2000 and implemented in January 2001. The reform includes a whole host of changes aimed at making the leave more generous and flexible. The two main objectives of the reform are to raise the take-up rate of parental leave among eligible families and to increase the proportion of fathers availing of the leave.[52] Under the new arrangements, father and mother can go on parental leave simultaneously. In addition, they both have the possibility of saving the third year of the parental leave period up until the child's eighth birthday. The maximum number of hours that a parent can work during parental leave has been increased from nineteen to thirty a week. Hence, if both parents are on parental leave simultaneously they can work up to sixty hours per week. In addition, parents on leave have a legal right to work part-time (between fifteen and thirty hours a week).[53] The reform also includes changes in the parental allowance scheme. The upper income limit for eligibility after six months is increased by 9.5 per cent for a two-parent family and by 11.4 per cent for a lone-parent family. Instead of receiving a parental allowance of a maximum of   307 a month up to the child's second birthday (an amount that has remained unchanged since the introduction of the allowance in 1986), parents are able to choose to receive an increased allowance up to the child's first birthday.

However, some parents, women's organisations and opposition parties have criticised the reform, claiming that it does not go far enough. The core of these criticisms has been that the public financial compensation for childcare is still not sufficient, as the amount has remained unchanged at €306.7 since payments were introduced for the first time in 1986 (European Industrial Relations Observatory).

Table 5 shows the five-country comparison as regards maternity, paternity and parental leave. There is clearly a huge degree of variation. In terms of generosity, whether this is interpreted to refer to duration, the amount of the payment, the upper age limit for children or all three, Sweden is in the vanguard while Ireland and the UK make up the rearguard. The absence of paid parental leave in these countries is the main reason for their relatively poor position.

Table 5: *Parental Leave Provision in Ireland, UK, Sweden, France and Germany (as of mid-2001)*

	Ireland	UK	Sweden	France	Germany
Basis of entitle- ment	individual	individual	mixed[a]	family	family
Duration	14 weeks	13 weeks	450 days	3 years	3 years
Age of child	0-5	0-5	0-8	0-3	0-8
Part-time work pos- sible	yes	yes	yes	yes	yes
Paid	no	no	yes	yes	yes
Monthly amount	-	-	80% wages + flat rate[#]	€485[~]	€306.7[**]
Period paid	-	-	450 days	3 years	2 years

a   The right is transferable between parents except for a 30-day period (for each)

\#   80 per cent gross salary is paid for 360 days

~   This is only available for second and subsequent children

**   This is only paid for low-income parents. Moreover, different income limits apply for the first 6 months and after the 7th month

4.4 Childcare Provision

4.4.1 Childcare Provision in the UK

Starting again with the UK, the picture is very similar to that of Ireland, both in terms of the available facilities and the national policy orientation. In the UK, state involvement in the provision of childcare has been minimal. Thus, successive governments have consistently emphasised the responsibility of parents to find and pay for daycare, except when children and families are in particular need of provision on the grounds of welfare or need.[54] With such a minimal state involvement in childcare and in the context of a growing demand for places (as women's labour participation continues to increase), most infrastructural developments have been market-led. However, the state has come under increasing pressure to become involved. This case has been pressed mainly by social and economic actors such as childcare and women's organisations, employers, trade unions and parents who regard the market as having failed to meet the needs of many families given scarce and unevenly distributed childcare provision as well as high costs. In response to these pressures, the Conservative government of John Major introduced new measures to tackle the problems of affordability and accessibility of childcare. These included tax exemptions to employers who were providing or subsidising childcare for their employees, a childcare voucher scheme (to the value of £1,100 (€1,791) a year) to help with the costs of early education for all four year olds, provisions to integrate early education and childcare and a childcare disregard for Family Credit.

These measures encountered but limited success. Since New Labour's accession to power, further steps have been taken towards increasing the level of good, affordable childcare. In 1998 the government published a National Childcare Strategy, a document which aimed to provide a framework for the provision of good quality, affordable childcare across the country. The main proposals included:

- the investment of £435 (€708) million in the development of childcare infrastructure (mainly designated for school-age childcare);

- the introduction of a Childcare Tax Credit alongside the Working Families' Tax Credit;

- the guarantee of a place in early education for all four-year-olds (whether in preschool or in centres traditionally seen as providing 'daycare' such as day nurseries[55]) and, in the longer term, three-year-olds;

- the transfer of responsibility for daycare from the Department of Health to the Department of Education and Employment.[56]

The current British government is of the view that these measures constitute both a demand- and supply-led approach, the Childcare Tax Credit being very important in the former regard. It is worth emphasising that New Labour abolished the Conservative's voucher scheme and in its first year in power set up the Early Years Development Plan. To be delivered through local partnerships consisting of public, private and voluntary providers, the target is to guarantee a place in preschool education to every four-year-old and eventually all three-year-olds. In order to avoid the failure of the former voucher scheme, grants are paid directly to private and voluntary providers. In 1998, with the publication of the National Childcare Strategy, it was proposed that Early Years Development Plans should be extended to cover childcare, becoming Early Years Development and Childcare Plans. This was seen as a further step towards the integration of daycare and early education. In addition, responsibility for daycare (previously in the hands of the Department of Health) was transferred to the Department of Education and Employment (which already held responsibility for preschool education).

These proposals, while much more in line with EU recommendations than those of successive Conservative governments, should be seen as an integral part of the

Welfare to Work policy. Thus, some of the proposals included in the strategy, such as those dealing with the problem of affordability of childcare, are primarily targeted at lone mothers and appear to result from evidence that lack of affordable childcare is keeping them from entering the workforce. Other proposals, mainly those dealing with the problem of 'accessibility' (such as the plans for the development of infrastructure) are to be delivered through local partnerships which include local authorities, the voluntary sector, business and parents. This is in line with the 1992 European Union Council Recommendation on Childcare. In general, although the degree of state involvement in childcare is greater than that in place ten years ago, the role assumed by government is that of an enabler and facilitator rather than a direct provider of services. The resemblance to Ireland in these and other regards is striking.

4.4.2 Childcare Provision in Sweden

Turning to Sweden, childcare there typically refers to care provided to children between the ages of one and five, although there are also extensive care arrangements for children of school age (up to twelve years). During the first one and a half years of life, most Swedish children are cared for at home while one of their parents is on parental leave. After that until they reach the age of compulsory schooling (six or seven years old), the vast majority receive municipal childcare. With respect to changes in childcare in Sweden, the 1990s can be divided into two distinct periods. The years between 1991 and 1994, coinciding with the peak of the economic crisis and a centrist coalition government, were characterised by the introduction of important savings measures and, in general, by a policy of creating incentives for the decentralisation and liberalisation of childcare. Greater decentralisation was effected by changing the grant system to the municipalities, from earmarked grants to general subsidies (in 1993). This gave local authorities more responsibility with respect to the organisation of childcare according to local needs. In addition, state subsidies to municipalities were significantly reduced and local income taxes were frozen between 1991 and 1994. A second policy goal in these first years of the 1990s was to diversify childcare. Hence for example in 1994, a flat-rate home care allowance of (2,000 SEK (€221.9) a month) was introduced as an alternative to municipal childcare, giving parents the option of looking after their children aged between one and three years at home. However, this allowance was abolished some months later (end of 1994) when the Social Democrats returned to power. Although for-profit provision of day care had been banned in 1988, during the 1991-1994 period the government provided incentives for the development of private childcare services by introducing special state grants for their establishment.

Policy changed in Sweden when the Social Democrats returned to power in 1995. While still moving towards a more 'welfare-mix' model, their policy was centred on the reinforcement of universalist principles governing Swedish social care. The main body of the current legislation concerning childcare was enacted in 1995 and 1998. In 1995, new legislation obliged local authorities to offer a place in childcare to all children aged between one and twelve years whose parents are working or studying or who have special needs. The law also specified requirements for the quality of the care provided. In 1996 the government sought to equalise provision across municipalities and county councils with the introduction of special state grants for those municipalities with lower levels of per capita taxable income. In the same year, responsibility for childcare services was transferred from the Ministry of Social Affairs to the Ministry of Education and in 1998 the regulations concerning childcare were transferred from the Social Services Act to the Education Act. This move has guaranteed standardisation of the content of preschool in all parts of the country. Later that year, preschool was included in the national educational curriculum, pointing to an increased emphasis on the pedagogical aspects of preschool activities. In 1999, the government announced a package of childcare measures primarily aimed at increasing the economic gain to paid work. These measures include: (a) the introduction of non-fee paying preschool for all children aged between four and five years of age, (b) the right of children aged between one and five years whose parents are unemployed to three hours per day of free preschool and (c) the introduction of fixed fees for public childcare.[57] Although these proposals affect all families with pre-school children, the reform is mainly targeted at parents working part-time and those who are unemployed.[58] The reform, introduced in different stages, began to take effect in July 2001 although the measures concerning childcare fees did not become operational until 2002.

4.4.3 Childcare Provision in France

Childcare provision in France is characterised by its:

- diversity, with a wide range of services, both collectively and individually provided;
- generosity, with a high degree of public financial support for each kind of service when viewed from a European perspective.

For most of the 1990s, policy effort was mainly geared towards the development of benefits for the payment of individual childcare, as against the provision of collective services. Economic factors played an important role in this, especially in the context of a serious deficit in the social security budget and high unemployment. However, in the past couple of years, childcare reforms have been primarily aimed at tackling the lack of sufficient places in collective childcare and at improving childcare choices for low-income parents.

As mentioned above, the main focus of policy attention in the 1990s was the introduction and/or revalorisation of childcare benefit programmes. The objective was to facilitate families to buy (individual) childcare services in the private sector, rather than to rely on the direct provision of services. Thus in 1998, total expenditure by the family fund of the social security (CNAF) on such childcare benefit schemes amounted to €1,544 million, in contrast to €755.2 million spent on public crèches. Since 1994, the single most widespread formal childcare arrangement for children aged under six years in France has taken the form of hiring the services of an approved childminder outside the home (21 per cent of children in this age group are cared for in this way). Towards this end, generous measures (including fiscal policy measures) aimed at the development of domestic employment were put in place. An allowance for hiring the services of a certified childminder was instituted in 1991. This allowance covers all social security contributions (regardless of income and family situation) associated with the employment of an approved childminder to care for a child under six years of age. In 1992 this allowance was supplemented by a flat-rate benefit, which was uprated in 1994 from €80.7 to €121.9. This led to a sharp increase in the number of recipients. Apart from this, allowance recipients can benefit from a deduction against tax of 25 per cent of total expenses incurred in childcare. This exists alongside a rather similar allowance giving assistance with employment costs involved in childcare, which was also improved during the 1990s. In existence since 1986, this (non means-tested) allowance partially covers the cost of the social security contributions involved in employing a domestic worker at home to care for children of up to three years of age. To be eligible, both parents must work. In 1994, the maximum amount of the allowance was doubled and extended to families with at least one child under six years of age. At the same time, the government tripled the amount of tax deductions (50 per cent of the costs of care up to an annual limit of €6,820).

These measures have had a mixed impact on the type of childcare to which French families with young children resort. On the one hand, there has been a considerable increase in the total use of paid childcare services, both collective and individual.[59] This is an important development in a country where informal childcare is still relatively widespread. On the other hand, the measures have been criticised for reinforcing unequal access to the different types of childcare arrangements since individual childcare is still too costly for low-income families. Thus, not surprisingly, the proportion of low-income families resorting to individual childcare is low when compared with their higher-income counterparts. It is appropriate therefore to speak of a class divide and of a stratification of services based on economic and social position: home help, financial subsidies and tax advantages for the wealthier households, crèches for the middle classes and mothers with stable employment, and local networks and intrafamilial help for the households with the lowest income (Letablier and Rieucau, 2000, p. 230).

However, in recent years, the Jospin government has tried to avoid the most negative aspects of this childcare policy by introducing some modifications. In 1998, the amount of social security payments and tax deductions allowed for employing a domestic worker to care for children under three years was significantly reduced for high income earning recipients. In 2001, the cash benefit for parents hiring the services of a certified childminder was increased by 48 per cent for low-income families and 23 per cent for families on average income, while it remained unchanged for high-income families. In the past couple of years, the government has substantially increased the investment in crèches and introduced a new system of subsidies primarily aimed at encouraging the development of crèches in disadvantaged areas.

4.4.4 Childcare Provision in Germany

In Germany the most important development in childcare policy during the decade was the implementation of the 1996 Childcare Act which granted each child between the ages of three and six the legal right to a place in *Kindergarten*.[60] This legislation was adopted in the context of a public debate around the introduction of further restrictions in the law on abortion and was consequently included in the maternal protection legislation (Pregnant Women and Family Assistance Amendment Law 1995). The legislation was regarded as providing better arrangements for working mothers and defined childcare as a protective measure for mothers and their unborn children – in the sense that no mother should have an abortion for non-medical reasons such as anticipated difficulties in combining work and childcare (Ostner, 1998, p. 131). Thus, the Childcare Act extended the concept of the *Kindergarten* – which had traditionally focused on the socialisation and educational aspects of childrearing rather than on supporting the labour market participation of mothers – to address the needs of mothers in reconciling work and family life (Meyer, 1994).

The local public youth welfare agencies are responsible for putting this legal right into effect: they should make available a place in *Kindergarten* for each child who is entitled to it and improve the supply of places available for children below the age of three and those in the compulsory schooling age range. However, the decision has put local authorities in former West Germany under considerable pressure with the result that services for children under three years and schoolchildren have been cut or not expanded. Furthermore, group size and/or the adult-children ratio in *Kindergarten* have been under pressure (Rostgaard and Fridberg, 1998, p. 513).

4.5 Provision for Care of the Elderly

4.5.1 Provision for the Care of the Elderly in the UK

The UK has seen huge changes in this regard. Successive Conservative governments in the 1980s sought to change the role of the social and health services from provider to enabler (facilitating and encouraging communities and clients to develop their own support system). These and other changes meant a rapid expansion of the independent sector of residential care and a shift in the meaning of community care (which increasingly came to refer to unpaid care delivered at home as opposed to professional services delivered in the community).

Since New Labour assumed government in 1997, the main thrust of the care policy introduced by the Conservatives has been maintained, although some new initiatives have been introduced. The most important of these are:

- the gradual recognition of informal carers and their inclusion in policy legislation. One important step in this direction had already been taken in 1995 with the Carers (Recognition and Services) Act, which gave carers the right to ask for a separate assessment of their needs. Since then, the New Labour government has drawn up a national strategy for carers which it published in 1999;

- the introduction and extension of direct payments by the local authorities giving care recipients the choice to make their own care arrangements.

In the past ten years, the number of local authority residential homes in the UK has gradually decreased at the same time as a very substantial growth has taken place in the number of residential homes in the hands of the independent sector. In fact the latter are currently the main providers of this type of care. This dramatic growth in private and voluntary residential care was partly the result of a rather generous social security package, in operation prior to 1993, available to Income Support recipients entering private or voluntary residential care. However, high costs led to the abolition of this provision in 1993. Today, local authorities rarely provide residential care themselves, yet they are responsible for making residential care arrangements for eligible claimants after an assessment of care needs has been carried out. Local authorities provide financial support to (previously assessed) claimants on condition that they satisfy a means test, with both claimants and their partners expected to make a contribution towards the fees. In recent years, there has been a significant growth in domiciliary services provided by the independent sector, although the degree of privatisation is not as stark as in residential and nursing care. Since the 1980s, domiciliary care provided or supported by local authorities has been increasingly restricted to the most dependent elderly people and this has been accompanied by the gradual disappearance of domestic assistance provision from many local authorities. As in Ireland, such care relies on and is supported by a network of informal care.

Social security payments to both carers and care recipients date back to the 1970s in the UK. The most recent innovation in payments for care was the introduction, in 1997, of direct payments by the local authorities. Reforms gave local authorities the discretion to make direct payments instead of services to people under sixty-five years who have been assessed as being in need of care. In February 2000 direct payments were extended to people aged over sixty-five (in England). The payments can be used to make one's own arrangements for care, such as employing a carer of one's choice.[61] The main financial support for informal carers is the Invalid Care Allowance, introduced in 1976 for men and single women of working age who gave up the opportunity of full-time work in order to care for a relative. In 1986, the benefit was extended to married women and non-relatives (to comply with EU equality law). Unlike Ireland, very few changes were made to this benefit in the UK in the 1990s. In 1994 the age limit for claiming was equalised at sixty-five years for men and women.[62] Since 1990 carers who are entitled to Income Support and in receipt of Invalid Care Allowance receive a special premium.

Recent changes in care policy for the elderly in the UK have been achieved through a greater reliance on informal networks of care. Yet, while informal care has been implicitly assumed in the policy making process, up until recently it had not been an explicit subject of legislation. In 1999, the New Labour government took an important step in the latter direction with the publication of a national strategy for carers. In line with the predominant view about the important role of the 'community' in social welfare, the document acknowledges the role of informal carers and explicitly proclaims the superiority of informal care over other forms of care. The strategy is novel in that it contains a policy package designed for carers. This package is very much in line with the overall Welfare to Work ideology, focusing on the relationship between the unpaid care work carried out in private households and the paid work carried out in the labour market. In line with this, it emphasises the need to support carers by way of:

- encouraging and enabling carers to remain in paid work: To this end, the family-friendly policies recently introduced by the government, especially the right to time off to deal with a family emergency in operation since December 1999, directly benefits carers. Apart from this, the government has introduced new incentives to employers to develop more generous leave of absence and flexible patterns of work.

- helping those carers who have withdrawn from the labour market to return to it after the caring period is over: To this end, the New Deal 50 Plus, introduced in April 2000, directly benefits carers the majority of whom are aged between forty-five and sixty years. This New Deal is designed for people aged fifty or over who have been out of work (due to unemployment, sickness/disability or caring responsibilities) for at least six months. It consists of the payment of so-called 'employment credits' (an extra £60 (€97.7) a week on top of wages) to beneficiaries taking a full-time job.

- protecting carers' pensions: Included in the strategy is a long-term plan to entitle carers to a second pension if they are: (a) either not working or with insufficient earnings to cross the lower earnings limit, and (b) receiving Invalid Care Allowance, or else caring for someone receiving Attendance Allowance, and if they qualify for a basic retirement pension protection scheme (Home Responsibilities Protection).

4.5.2 Provision for the Care of the Elderly in Sweden

In Sweden, where care policy for the elderly is more established, the 1990s saw fewer changes than either the UK or Ireland. Those changes that were implemented were more in the practice of eldercare (in particular, changes in the interpretation of existing policy) than changes in policy. Several observers are of the view that the changes in the practice of eldercare point towards a departure from the universalist principle of the Swedish model of social services.

The most important policy change is the 1992 Adel reform which, in giving municipalities the responsibility for both health care and social care of the elderly, represents a step towards increased decentralisation of eldercare. Previously, the county councils were responsible for health and medical care while social services were run by the municipalities. The 1992 reform made municipalities responsible for institutional housing and care facilities, health care within institutional housing and care facilities (not including care provided by physicians) as well as giving them financial responsibility for hospital 'bed-blockers' in acute somatic hospital care and geriatric clinics. The reform also included the provision of incentive grants for municipalities to improve the quality of housing for the elderly.[63]

The Swedish Social Services Act (introduced in 1982 and revised in 1998), which regulates home help, states that a person who needs help in managing everyday tasks has a right to assistance if the need cannot be met in any other way. However, this piece of legislation can and has been interpreted in different ways. In recent years, some municipalities have interpreted it so that the right would apply only to the oldest, most frail, poorest and most isolated of elderly people, while the rest are encouraged to find alternative care either in the market or within the family. Hence in recent years, home-help services have devoted more time to personal care than household chores. The definition of 'need' has been made much more restrictive so that requiring help with cleaning or shopping (as opposed to help in getting up, bathing, and so forth) does not make one eligible for home help. In line with this general trend, user charges for home-help services have been increased. It is estimated that the average charge tripled between 1989 and 1994, at the same time that fees were more closely related to income. As a consequence, for those who require lower levels of help, it is often cheaper to buy those services in the private market (Szebehely, 1999). Thirdly, the eligibility principle is being further altered by the introduction of family considerations into eligibility assessments. Thus, for example, older people who have children living nearby are less likely to receive home help than those without children or those whose children are living far away. Also, it has become common practice for organisers in charge of assessing the need for home-help to investigate whether the claimant has anyone close by who can provide the care required (Szebehely, 1999). Finally, some means testing has been introduced. Hence, an increasing number of municipalities do not provide home helps to those with an income above the social assistance level.

4.5.3 Provision for the Care of the Elderly in France

French social care for the elderly has yet to see anything comparable to the massive development of childcare provision of past years. Social care for the elderly is very different from that for children in other ways as well. For one, it is marked in France by an absence of central state support. Since its decentralisation in 1984, care for the elderly is the concern of county authorities (*Departements*). This has led to great regional disparities. In a second departure from childcare, provision for the elderly is funded from a number of sources. Along with the *Departements*, funding is also provided by the numerous social security pension funds (depending on the recipient's pension scheme). A lack of communication between the different sources of finance has been said to be a major obstacle to the development of services (Thierry and Palach, 1999). Thirdly, all types of aid for care of the elderly are governed by a means test. This applies to both aid provided by the *Departements* (which is actually limited to those below the poverty line) as well as that provided by the different pension funds.

Looking at trends over the 1990s, two are common to both childcare and elderly care policies: an emphasis on financial aid for care needs rather than on the direct provision of services; the introduction of incentives aimed at the development of domestic employment. Thus, in the past ten years the most significant developments in policy on care for the elderly have been the creation of a benefit for the very dependent elderly (*Prestation Spécifique Dépendence* – PSD) and a number of schemes of social security exemptions and tax deductions for those aged over seventy years to hire a domestic assistant. The PSD benefit was introduced in 1997 for people of at least sixty years of age who are heavily dependent (living either at home or in a care institution). It replaced another general benefit for disabled people (no age specification) which was introduced in 1975. PSD is a means-tested benefit, financed by local departments (*Conseils Généraux*) and can be paid directly to the beneficiary (on condition that 90 per cent of the amount is used to pay for care), to a home-care service organisation or to an institution. The amount varies according to the degree of dependence, which is calculated on the basis of a national grid,[64] the claimant's resources and place of residence (i.e. whether at home or in an institution).

4.5.4 Provision for the Care of the Elderly in Germany

Of all the four countries, Germany saw the most far-reaching changes in regard to eldercare during the 1990s. In 1995 social insurance for long-term care was introduced. Prior to this, the possibility of receiving financial support with the costs of care and assistance for dependent elderly people was limited so that most home care was provided by family members.[65] People in need of care beyond the unpaid help of family members had to either pay for it themselves or apply for means-tested social assistance which covered some of the costs of long-term care.[66] In the latter case though, their entitlement would be determined only after the means of their adult children had been examined. Their only other alternative was to try and get themselves defined as in need of medical treatment in order to have the costs of care services covered by the health insurance. With a growing population of frail elderly people in need of care and a rising expenditure on social assistance care benefits and provisions, local governments and the Länder (then in charge of financing social assistance) appealed for the costs of eldercare to be shifted between levels of government (Ostner, 1998, p. 121). Legislation introducing the long-term care insurance was passed by the German parliament in 1994, establishing compulsory contributions for long-term care from all those covered by either statutory or private sickness insurance (dependent children and spouses are covered by the insurance without contributions if their own income does not exceed a set limit).[67]

The principal aims of the scheme are (Rostgaard and Fridberg, 1998, p. 523):

• to keep people in need of care in their own homes for as long as possible;

• to reduce the need for placements in residential care;

• to stimulate and activate social networks around those in need of care;

• to make people in need of care independent of social assistance.

The scheme allows a choice between care services, cash payments or a combination of both. Cash payments may be used to pay family members, neighbours, or to purchase care from for-profit or non-profit providers. Care services may be provided either at home or in a residential institution.

4.6 Children's Rights

During the 1990s, children's rights received a lot of publicity. The 1989 UN Convention on the Rights of the Child, which has now been ratified by all countries in the world except for the United States and Somalia, has undoubtedly exerted a significant influence on recent policy developments. It has been especially significant in:

• putting a new focus on children's participatory rights. This has led to the establishment of new mechanisms enabling children's voices to be heard, such as children's parliaments, children's ombudsmen, consultation exercises with children during the policy-making process, and so forth.

• a new focus on parental responsibilities and on the state's obligation to support parents in fulfilling these, leading in many cases to the reform of family law and also to the development of parenting support services.

However, there are important variations in how the Convention is being implemented across Europe. An analysis of these variations is revealing insofar as implementation of the Convention does not take place in a vacuum but in the context of varying policy and institutional traditions.

4.6.1 Children's Rights in the UK

In the UK, the Convention has been in force since 1992, although successive governments have been slow in implementing it. In recent years, child policy has been characterised by a strong focus on parental responsibility, while paying little attention to children's participatory rights. This stands in stark contrast to developments in other countries such as Sweden, France and, most recently, Ireland.

The move towards a greater focus on parental responsibility is a common trend in all five countries studied in this report (a trend which has led to family law reform in many of them). One of the clearest examples of this trend in the UK is the fact that the child maintenance scheme, introduced in 1992, figures amongst the strictest in Europe (as described under 4.2.1 above). However, the UK is a case apart in that this trend extends beyond the reinforcement of parental responsibilities in the upbringing of children to include responsibilities for the children's 'adequate' socialisation. Put differently, in the UK parents are not only seen as the primary carers and educators of children but they are also held responsible should their children engage in 'anti-social' behaviour. An example illustrating this is the reform of juvenile justice carried out in 1998 (Crime and Disorder Act 1998). The reform brought new interventions and structures, including new parenting orders requiring that parents of young offenders undergo regular classes in parenting skills, impose child curfews and ensure that their children attend school regularly. Failure to comply can result in conviction and fines of up to £1,000 (€1,629).

This strong emphasis on parental responsibility is also reflected in early intervention initiatives aimed at tackling social exclusion, whereby social exclusion is conceptualised in close relation to 'inadequate parenting'. For example, one of the main components of Sure Start – the main early intervention programme targeted at very young disadvantaged children – is parenting education.

Children's participatory rights have been given little attention until very recently. In contrast to initiatives already taken in Ireland, Germany, Sweden and France, there are no mechanisms in place to enable children to participate in policy matters that most affect them (such as a children's parliament, local children's councils). In the past couple of years, though, some progress has begun to take place, especially with regard to children's participation in the policy making process through consultation exercises. In 2000, a Children's and Young People's Unit was set up to support work on children and young people across government departments. The unit was also assigned the task of developing a national strategy for children and young people in England. In preparing the strategy, the unit has carried out extensive consultation with children and young people of different ages.

The UK has also been slow in setting up an independent monitoring system (children's ombudsman or children's commissioner) to make sure that the Convention is properly implemented. Currently in place in Ireland, France and Sweden, the appointment of independent officers has been urged by the Committee on the Rights of the Child[68] and promoted by the Council of Europe in its 1996 Recommendation on a European Strategy for Children. Although the roles of the Children's Ombudsman vary from country to country, they generally include:

- promoting government compliance with the Convention;
- promoting awareness and understanding of children's rights;
- promoting effective co-ordination of government on children at all levels;
- providing a channel for children's views of policy, encouraging both government and the public to give proper respect to children's views;
- assisting with or initiating legal proceedings and investigations into abuses of children's rights;

- ensuring that children have an effective means of compensation when their rights are violated.

In 1995, the UK's failure to establish independent mechanisms to support and protect children's human rights was severely criticised by the Committee. However, the devolutionary process has enabled Northern Ireland, Wales and Scotland to move closer towards establishing their own Children's Commissioners. Thus, the Welsh Assembly appointed its first Children's Commissioner in 2000, while both the Northern Ireland Assembly and the Scottish Parliament have agreed on the need to appoint a Children's Commissioner in the near future.[69] No such moves towards the establishment of a Children's Commissioner have as yet been taken in England.[70]

4.6.2 *Children's Rights in Sweden*

In contrast to the UK, Sweden is regarded as a pioneering country in the field of children's rights. Not alone has child policy moved towards a stronger focus on children's participatory rights but the government has adopted a 'whole child perspective' in regard to all policies that have an impact on children (e.g. social security, health, education, environment, justice, urban planning, and so forth). Apart from this, significant progress has been made in the field of research into the conditions of children and the development of child statistics.

Sweden was one of the first countries where the UN Convention on the Rights of the Child entered into force (1990). Three years later, a Children's Ombudsman was established with the task of safeguarding the rights and interests of children as laid down in the Convention. Since then, the Ombudsman has been involved in a variety of activities, including:

- monitoring the implementation of the Convention within the municipalities;
- promoting participation of children within the munici-palities;

- producing and distributing information on the Convention and its interpretation;
- compiling annual statistics on the conditions of children and young persons;
- facilitating a dialogue with children through the Ombudsman's website and school-based seminars.

Sweden is a highly de-centralised country and therefore the most important activities involving children and young persons take place at a local level (i.e. municipalities and county councils). Local decision making makes it possible for children and young persons to be actively involved in the settling of questions which in various ways concern them. Towards this end, a number of municipalities have set up youth councils and youth parliaments.

In recent years, the most significant development in the field of children's rights was the introduction of a whole child perspective in all relevant government policies. In the 1998 Programme for Government, the prime minister stated that the Convention should permeate all decision making within government offices that affect children. A year later, a strategy for the implementation of the UN Convention was agreed in parliament. According to the strategy report, the chief aim is to develop the capacity of adult society to listen to children and to perceive the effects of different decisions on children. Under the new strategy, national, regional and local authorities are to observe and apply the Convention in the course of their activities. This involves, inter alia, the introduction of child impact assessments in all decisions affecting children, the adoption of a child perspective in the terms of reference for government commissions, the establishment of monitoring systems in municipalities and county councils, and the further development of child statistics (Government of Sweden, 1998).

4.6.3 Children's Rights in France

In France, the implementation of children's rights has followed a pattern that while initially different from that of the UK has recently come to resemble the approach adopted there. That is, during the first half of the decade, implementation of the Convention mainly focused on the development of children's participatory rights but in recent years the focus has shifted to the re-inforcement of parental responsibilities and the development of mechanisms of parental support.

Like Sweden, France ratified the Convention in 1990 and soon after a number of institutions enabling the participation of children in public life were set up. Thus, since the early 1990s children have been able to participate in local government through children's local councils established throughout the communes. In 2000, more than 400 councils were in place. Apart from this, a National Children's Parliament was introduced in 1994. The parliament, which meets every year, allows children to vote on a new piece of legislation (previously proposed by them) in relation to issues that most affect them.[71] This legislation then becomes part of the law of the French Republic.[72] In addition, a Children's Ombudsman (*Defenseur des Enfants)* was established in 2000 with the mission of promoting children's rights, dealing with individual complaints of children whose rights have not been respected, and making proposals for law in the area of children's rights to the parliament. In particular the Office is involved in a number of activities such as:

- influencing policy development at national level;
- collecting data on children;
- monitoring the impact of laws on children;
- monitoring the implementation of the Convention;
- dealing with individual cases;
- training professionals and other groups on children's rights.

While the main developments in children's participatory rights took place during the first half of the 1990s, policy in the last couple of years has mainly focused on those articles of the Convention that deal with parental rights and responsibilities and the state's obligation to support parents in fulfilling their role. Thus, parental obligations have been re-inforced through a reform of family law aimed at promoting joint custody of the child after separation or divorce. At the same time, the state has made significant investment in the development of programmes specifically aimed at supporting parents in their role of primary carers and educators of children.

4.6.4 Children's Rights in Germany

In Germany, the implementation of children's rights has followed a similar pattern to those taking place in France, especially in recent years. As in France, German family law has been recently reformed with a view to strengthening parental responsibility in the education and upbringing of children (Law of Parent and Child 1998). The new law promotes joint custody for parents, while adopting the principle of consideration of the best interest of the child as the chief procedural principle under family law. Hence, while the reform enables parents to continue exercising joint custody after separation or divorce, in cases where an older child is involved (fourteen years or older), his or her wishes are taken into consideration. Also similar to France, the reform has been accompanied by the development of mechanisms aimed at supporting parents in their roles of carers and educators of children. For example, in recent years the government has adopted a new policy approach towards child and youth services by focusing them more on family support. This new approach involves the provision of parenting-skills courses and similar support services.

With respect to children's participatory rights, these are, as in France and Sweden, well developed although, unlike those two countries, Germany still lacks a children's rights' institution (ombudsman or parliament) operating at national level. The spectrum of participatory models in Germany's Länder and municipalities varies widely, ranging from child commissioners to institutionalised and direct forms of participation such as children's parliaments, children's councils or round tables. These institutions exist at the municipal level in all of the Länder. Apart from this, a number of Länder are supporting participatory approaches by enshrining participatory rights for children in their local government codes and education Acts. Another form of participation is through consultation exercises. In this respect, several NGOs have held consultations all over the country to give children an opportunity to indicate which rights they consider most important. One innovation not shared by any of the other countries studied in this report is that, in five German Länder, the minimum voting age in local elections has been lowered from eighteen to sixteen years. Finally, following similar initiatives already in place in Sweden, the government has recently made a commitment to introduce child impact assessments in all matters of relevance to the child and to develop a child policy as a distinct policy area.

4.7 Overview of Trends in Family Policy During the 1990s

Looking beyond the details and fine print of reform, it is possible to summarise these and other complex developments by saying that family policy in these five countries has been characterised by the following landmark developments over the last decade.

4.7.1 A Redefinition of Family

There is taking place a general redefinition of family, involving a move to focus on the obligations of parenthood as distinct from conjugal ties. Family solidarity is being reinterpreted and redefined to refer to parental responsibility rather than spouses or partners' solidarity towards each other (Letablier and Rieucau, 2000, p. 221). One can think of policy as 'activating' parenthood and parenting. It is in this light that the developments around emphasising and enforcing the responsibilities of absent fathers should be read. Another example of the active parenting link is the 'daddy leave' introduced by the Swedish government. In regard to parental leave generally, its relationship to equality resembles a Catch 22. If parental leave were taken equally by women and men, it would promote gender equality; however for it to be taken equally gender equality must already be in place (Moss and Deven, 1999, pp. 13-14).

Overall, given the weakening of marital ties and the diversification of forms of private life, European countries are finding it judicious to focus on parental obligations and relations since these outlast the break-up of conjugal ties. This is not (yet) an observable trend in Ireland, mainly because the instability of marriage is not so advanced.

4.7.2 A Move Towards Children's Rights

A second visible trend is towards granting children autonomous rights. This is in some ways a further manifestation of the trend towards individualisation but it also draws on a more general concern about the wellbeing of children. There is also much empirical evidence of this trend – for example, the guarantee of a place in childcare as a right for children in the UK, Germany and Sweden.[73] This is in stark contrast to earlier social policies which were for long active (although not alone) in consolidating a conventional set of images of children as dependent. Earlier policies familialised children, defining them as 'minors' and 'dependants' of adults. In Makrinioti's view, welfare state policies have played a significant role in perpetuating the notion of childhood as a minority status and in concealing its social visibility by supporting and reinforcing children's familialisation (1994, p. 268). As a result, it has been difficult to see children apart from the family and indeed the industrialised world has been accused by Therborn (1993) of missing the opportunity to make the twentieth century the 'century of the child'. One could definitely say of policy in the past that it assumed that the interests of children were identical and inseparable from those of parents and guardians. In fact there was a strong sense in which children were regarded as the property of their parents. This helps to explain why most countries have been caught unawares by the scale of child abuse and why it has to be perceived as a 'crisis' once it is discovered. Not alone is trust shattered by child abuse on a wide scale but the founding pillars of much of the social architecture are rendered unstable. Once the knowledge of child abuse is absorbed into policy, a far-reaching change of approach is required (although it is not automatic): children come to be conceived of as separate to adults, as having interests, these interests begin to be demarcated from those of adults and the state begins to lay out minimum requirements for the child's wellbeing (Whyness, 2000, p. 40).

In fact, a number of different approaches to or discourses of children are still to be found in most European countries. The continuum of approaches tends to co-exist in each national setting. One discourse is that of control. This, found especially in educational policy, rests on the assumption that, since children lack self-control, they need to be regulated (Stainton Rogers, 2001, p. 30). Although it still underlies much policy, the control view is less widely endorsed today as compared with former times. A second discourse is that of child welfare. This is perhaps the most familiar discourse, being especially prevalent in contemporary social policy. Its departure point is that children need protection and that they are entitled to a 'good childhood' (Stainton Rogers). Policies underpinned by this viewpoint construct children as the passive recipients of adult protection. This means that parents' rights are usually placed ahead of those of children, if the latter are considered in their own right at all (Lansdown, 2001, p. 90). This kind of approach is rendered vulnerable by the now undeniable facts that adults (including parents) do not always act in children's best interests and that they may indeed abuse their power over children. A third discourse perceives the child as an individual. In this discourse terms like the 'child's best interests' begin to make an appearance. This has a number of dimensions and seems to take the form of a progressive line of development rather than being achieved in one go. The core understanding is that children's welfare is no longer realised by giving adults rights over them but rather by an adherence to the human rights' standards defined by international law (and the UN Convention on the Rights of the Child in particular) (Lansdown, p. 97). The end point is children as citizens with rights. This is realised through a number of different steps or stages. A fundamental aspect is an emphasis on children's right to knowledge which in turn strengthens their capacity to make informed choices (Whyness, 2000, p. 128). A second emphasis is on children participating in areas that have always been defined as the province of adult authority (Whyness, pp. 128-9). One overall effect is for the boundaries between adulthood and childhood to become less fixed. One could use the term 'children's policy' for this kind of approach: policy is focused on children as a specific group in society as distinct from the family, women, the labour market or the community (Ruxton, 2001, p. 69).

Ireland's National Children's Strategy is quite close to the last position. Moreover, it is set in a context whereby recent developments in child-related family legislation have been said to represent a significant shift from the traditional adult-centred nature of the law (Martin, 2000, p. 58). If one takes Euronet's (1999) criteria for an emerging and enlightened 'children's policy', the recently-announced strategy appears in a very positive light (Figure 1).

Figure 1: Evaluating Ireland's National Children's Strategy
according to Euronet's Criteria for a Good
Children's Policy

Criteria	National Children's Strategy
The best interests of the child as a guiding principle	
Increasing investment in children and ensuring fair distribution of resources among social groups	
Overall co-ordination of policy, based on cross-departmental working to agreed strategies	
Policies addressing both the direct and indirect interests of children	
The systematic collection of information on children to identify their needs and policy priorities	
The establishment of independent bodies to monitor children's rights	
The participation of children in decision making, both within the family and beyond	

It will be interesting to observe how this policy is realised and whether it leads to significant change in other policy domains which at this stage in Ireland remain much closer to the first and second discourses.

4.7.3 Supporting Working (among) Parents

A further trend, in Ireland and elsewhere, is for the expansion of supports to working parents (as indicated by the growth in maternity and parental leave provisions). Gauthier (1999) provides a lot of evidence in support of this trend. She also points out that, while families have not benefited from a major reduction in the direct costs of children, they have benefited from a significant reduction in the indirect (or opportunity) costs. Mothers are especially targeted in the desire for greater numbers of working families. We have seen evidence of this in the way in which lone parents in some countries, the UK especially, are strongly encouraged to be economically active. The employment of mothers was for long a concern and a policy objective in the Scandinavian countries. While policy makers and the public in Ireland are accustomed to viewing the matter in terms of 'enabling mothers to be employed', the issue is framed in Scandinavia in terms of 'enabling workers to be mothers and, increasingly, fathers'. This trend towards supporting workers as parents is very much in line with the general 'activation' thrust of cash benefits throughout Europe (which is strongly supported by the EU). Some would be critical of this trend. For it also raises the question of the meaning of the very widely-used phrase 'reconciling work and family' and especially questions the relative emphases given to family and work. Measures that are framed within a discourse of reconciling work and home appear much more as supports of employment than of family.

4.7.4 Supporting Families with the Indirect Costs of Children

When the growth in parental leave is taken together with the big expansion of subsidies and/or allowances for childcare, one of the most significant developments in Europe is a move towards assisting families with the indirect costs of children. Hence, while families have not benefited from a major reduction in the direct costs of children, they have been helped with the indirect (or opportunity) costs (Gauthier, 1999). There is a danger that the two forms of costs are being treated as substitutable though, apart from Ireland, child benefits are not being raised substantially.

One of the questions about this set of developments is how it is linked to anti-poverty policy and social equity. Much of the original impetus for family policy sprung from an anti-poverty orientation. Now the view is becoming more widespread that poverty is the result of a family's insufficient attachment to the labour market. As a result, some of the anti-poverty function is being shifted to fiscal policy, especially in the UK, and there is growing acceptance of the legitimacy of the activation focus of social policy. It is difficult to see how child benefits can thrive under this ideology.

But there are also matters of equity. What is most at issue in this regard is a tension if not clash between horizontal and vertical equity. We know that the former was an important motivator of family benefits especially in the continental European countries. The 1990s have seen a tension between these two principles or goals in a number of countries, at its most volatile perhaps in France where the Jospin government was forced to overturn its policy to subject the family benefits to a means test (in 1998) after only a few months. In this instance horizontal equity won out. There is another equity aspect involved – which families can afford to accept the increasingly diverse forms of help available? This comes up in relation to the next trend.

4.7.5 A Move to a Welfare Mix Approach

Whereas in the past a unidimensional form of social provision was acceptable, now the values of global capitalism are inculcating notions of choice and diversity in regard to all aspects of life. The effects are widely-felt. In the sphere of social benefits and services, there is a growing feeling that one form of provision is insufficient. This is especially the case in countries where the state has traditionally been a strong service provider. State-dominated provision is said not only to curtail choice but to be inferior to the market which is portrayed as efficient, competitive, profit maximising and rational. This kind of thinking opens the way to market provision as well as portraying family provision as a form of freedom and choice. The 1990s were a time in Europe when family-related and other policy traditions were (capable of) being rewritten. The notion of 'collective' (usually public) provision was being undermined in favour of individualised, personalised services. In relation to France for example, Letablier and Rieucau (2000) speak of a general movement towards individualisation and privatisation of action wherein the norms of the market and of individual choice are widely supported. The conception of childcare as a public issue has been transformed in France, so much so that these authors speak of a dissolution of a national consensus regarding an ideal of childhood and of equal opportunity. In France the crèche represented not just a conception of the appropriate way of bringing up children but stood for a certain form of equal opportunities for children which was in turn part of the realisation of the common good. Now class differentiation begins to make its appearance – with the wealthier opting for a different form of provision (almost always a service that is 'bought' (even at low cost)) whereas the crèches are more and more servicing the children of the working classes.

Chapter 5

Learning from Policy: Impacts Associated with Family Policy

This report's final empirical task is to identify impacts associated with family policy. Rather than the goals, objectives or principles of policy, this part of the research focuses on outcomes associated with particular policy approaches adopted in Ireland and elsewhere. To ascribe particular effects to policies is a risky endeavour, not least because of measurement and methodological difficulties. Identifying definite effects requires a kind of experimental approach wherein one keeps constant all other factors apart from the policy itself. Obviously in social situations this level of control of variables is impossible. Hence one cannot define the task at hand in terms of identifying 'effects' in the manner in which that term is normally understood. The notion of 'associated impact' is more appropriate. To identify these, the results of research on the general impact of policies that are in place will be examined.

One way of organising the study of associated policy impacts is to think of policies as influencing both resources and behaviours. Following Barbier (1990, p.335), this chapter differentiates between two general types of impact: the distribution of income and behavioural effects. The effects on financial resources are the most direct (and probably identifiable) of all policy impacts. To identify these, the degree of horizontal redistribution and the extent of poverty among families with children will be traced. Turning to the behavioural effects, two are especially interesting. The first is family size (effectively fertility rates) and the second is labour market participation patterns especially of mothers.

A few words are apposite at the outset about the data and methodology. In the first instance, it should be pointed out that examination of its effects or associated outcomes always lags considerably behind policy. One has to wait for the data to become available (and sometimes specially designed studies are needed). Hence it is important to note that most of the research examined in this chapter may not relate to current policy.

As regards methodology, existing research has used a number of different methods to identify the impact of policy on the family. Among these is the model family method, which uses model families to compare the distribution of income in deciles before and after social transfers. The choice of types of families is somewhat open but usually family types are chosen to represent family size, the presence of one or two parents, the number of earners and income level. One of the best-known applications of this method is a study by Bradshaw et al (1993) which sought to compare the generosity of provision for families with children in a large number of countries. Atkinson, Bourguignon and Chiappori (1987) adopted a somewhat different method in attempting to identify the effects of the UK system of benefits and taxation, by modelling it on other national samples. Both of these appear to be very particular methods which have limited benefits. For one, both consider only the income effects of cash transfers and tax allowances. In addition, the model family method is limited in the number of different family types it can assess while the method used by Atkinson, Bourguignon and Chiappori is suitable mainly for studying the operation of one benefit system (rather than five as in the present case). Hence in the interests of diversity and complexity, it is more appropriate to identify the range of effects discussed above. There is another reason also to conceive of the effects of policy in a broad way – our study is not limited to cash benefits or taxation but includes also service provision relating to the care of children and the elderly.

5.1 Horizontal Redistribution

The principal instruments of horizontal redistribution in tax and benefit systems are:

* universal family allowances (child benefit);
* joint taxation of spouses;
* tax allowances and/or credits for married couples, children and lone parents.

The type of instruments used, and the relevance of each in relation to others, varies widely across the five countries under study.

Ireland operates a system of optional joint taxation (of the aggregation type)[74] and tax allowances for lone parents (so that their total personal allowance equals that of married couples). The system of joint taxation is, however, increasingly being questioned with more emphasis placed on supporting children through the benefit system. Thus, for example, there have been proposals to eliminate joint taxation and replace it with a special child benefit for children under the age of three years. In addition, the value of the universal child benefit – traditionally one of the least generous in Europe – has been increased significantly in recent years. Another trend is for the recognition for financial purposes of the unpaid work of home carers: in 2000 a new Home Carer's Allowance was introduced for families where the woman is mainly working at home, with an estimated average value of €12.6 a week (Plumb and Walsh, 2000, p. 60).

In the UK, supporting children through the tax and benefit system is increasingly favoured as an instrument of horizontal redistribution rather than, say, the support of married couples and lone parents. Although joint taxation was abolished in the 1970s, up until very recently tax credits were available for married couples and lone parents. The real value of these, however, was very small and the credits were finally abolished in the year 2000. However, the new Working Families' Tax Credit involves a return to joint taxation for claimant families. The value of child benefit was increased in recent years and a new Children's Tax Credit – significantly more generous than the recently abolished married couples and lone parent allowances – was introduced in Spring 2001.

In Sweden, the main mechanism of horizontal redistribution is the universal child benefit, although public services also play a very important role in supporting families. Taxation is used exclusively as a mechanism of vertical redistribution. Hence joint taxation and/or tax relief for spouses, lone parents and/or children do not exist.

Of the five countries under study, France is the only one to operate a system of compulsory joint taxation for couples and their children (*Quotient Familial*).[75] This is a type of family taxation whereby family size (in contrast to Germany and Ireland) is taken into account in the calculation of taxes by the inclusion of each dependent child in the formula. Lone parents are taxed as married couples. Apart from this, there are also cash allowances for families with two or more children (*Allocations Familiales*), with generous increases for each additional child. Furthermore, families with three or more children also receive a benefit supplement (*Complément Familial*) which, although subject to a means test, is received by 85 per cent of these families.

Germany has a system of optional joint taxation (of the income splitting type).[76] Apart from this, there are child benefits (*Kindergeld*) or tax allowances (*Kinderfreibetraege*) for dependent children and allowances for lone parents.[77] Tax credits for children are paid out by private and public employers in the form of a monthly tax refund. However, parents who are not subject to income tax liability receive their Kindergeld payment as a monthly social security benefit paid directly by the public authorities.

Studies comparing the generosity of policy packages aimed at horizontal redistribution across different countries tend to use the model family method. One of the most recent comparative studies done on this subject at a European level was carried out by the European Observatory on National Family Policies in 1996.[78] The aim of the study was to compare the structure and value of the child benefit package, including (a) child tax allowances/credits, (b) child benefits (universal and/or means-tested), (c) social assistance payable to low income families, (d) child income support for lone parents, and (e) child maintenance advances paid from public funds. The value of the child benefit package was expressed as the difference in purchasing power parities (in ECU) between the net income[79] of a childless couple and that of a couple, with children, with the same earnings[80]. The model families used in the study were: couple and lone parent families in employment, with varying numbers of children, at five different earnings' levels.[81]

In relation to the five countries examined in this report, the following are some of the results yielded by the analysis of the European Observatory study (1998).

For large, low-income families (one-earner family with three children on half average male earnings), the child benefit package[82] is highest in France, very closely followed by Sweden. In both of these countries, large families are especially favoured by the child benefit/family allowance provisions. Furthermore, in France these families qualify for a means-tested child benefit supplement. These two countries are followed in relative generosity by the UK and Ireland. Despite the fact that the amount of the universal child benefit is lowest in Ireland, both the UK and Ireland have means-tested benefits available for low-income families, the overall amount of which is higher than that of the universal child benefit (particularly in Ireland). Lastly, the value of the child benefit package for a large, low-income family is lowest in Germany, despite the fact that this country has the most generous universal child benefit scheme.

For high-income, dual-earner families with two children (1.5 average male earnings and 1.5 average female earnings), the value of the child benefit package is again highest in France. This time, though, France is very closely followed by Germany. Despite the fact that there is no child benefit for the first child in France, there are very generous tax allowances for families with children (through the system of the *Quotient Familial*) which especially benefit higher-income families. As indicated above, Germany has the most generous child benefit scheme of the five countries under study. These countries are then followed by Sweden and the UK. It is worth noting that in both of the latter countries the amount of the universal child benefit is higher than in France, yet their tax systems do not contain any mechanism of horizontal redistribution to favour high-income families with children (child tax allowances, for example). Lastly, the amount of the child benefit package for a high-income, dual-earner family was lowest in Ireland. As indicated above, the universal child benefit in this country is low compared with the other countries in the study. Furthermore, Ireland's tax system does not offer tax allowances for children (which would especially benefit this type of family).

Analysis of the value of the child benefit package for families on average earnings by number of children allows one to assess the impact of an extra child on the disposable income of a family. In the study under consideration, such analysis yielded the following results for the following families on average male earnings:

- for families with one child, the value of the package is highest in Germany, followed by the UK, and is lowest in France and Ireland (note that the UK is the only country where child benefit is higher for the first child);

- for families with two children, the value is again highest in Germany, but this time followed by Sweden, and is lowest in France and Ireland;

- for families with three children the value is highest in France, followed by Sweden. The UK and Ireland make up the rear.

Overall, Ireland fares rather poorly in these comparisons. Note, however, that the research by the European Observatory on National Family Policies does not take account of the very significant increases in child benefit in Ireland since the mid-1990s. Given such increases, Ireland's relative position is likely to compare more favourably in the present time (because it saw such a large increase while in the other countries, apart from the UK, the value of child and family benefits remained more or less stable).

5.2 Poverty Among Families with Children

Recent research estimating child poverty at the mid-1990s shows that, of the five countries under study, the UK has the highest incidence of child poverty while Sweden has the least (Innocenti Research Centre, 2000). However, Ireland also emerges as a high child poverty country, it is ranked fourth out of the five countries with poverty rates of between 17 and 21 per cent.[83]

Table 6:   Relative and Absolute Child Poverty Rates in Ireland, UK, Sweden, France and Germany (mid-1990s)

Country	Year	% of children living in households below the poverty line			
		50% national median*		US official poverty line#	
		Rate	Rank	Rate	Rank
Ireland	1997	16.8	4	21.4	4
UK	1995	19.8	5	29.1	5
Sweden	1995	2.6	1	5.3	1
France	1994	7.9	2	10.7	2
Germany	1994	10.7	3	12.5	3

Source: Innocenti Research Centre (2000).

*   Poverty here is defined as households with income below 50 per cent of the national median accross the entire population.

\#   This is an absolute poverty measure set at US$15,299 for a couple and two children in 1995.

What are the social and economic correlates of child poverty?

As regards child poverty and lone motherhood, some of the five countries have both high rates of lone motherhood and high child poverty, the UK especially. Apart from this, evidence shows that in almost all the countries children of lone mothers have a greater poverty risk than children in two-parent households. However, variations in lone motherhood cannot account for the variation in overall child poverty rates across countries. Thus for example, Sweden has high rates of lone motherhood but low rates of child poverty while Italy has low rates of lone motherhood but high rates of child poverty.

In general, there is a significant relationship between the proportion of GNP spent on social expenditure and child poverty rates. But, assuming that social expenditure plays a crucial role in the variation in child poverty, it would be reasonable to expect that the link with poverty would be stronger if one could identify income transfers going to families likely to fall into poverty. However, there is only a weak relationship between poverty and targeted transfers. Hence, the UK and Ireland have high transfers of this type but also high poverty rates while Sweden has very low levels of targeted transfers but also low poverty rates.

Clearly, one must place social welfare provisions within a broader context. In relation to children, poverty and their wellbeing, Sorensen's (1999) comparison of the USA, Sweden, Italy and Germany indicates that the instability of families in the 'post-nuclear family age' has high costs for children, especially if the economic consequences of single parenthood are substantial. The new family form which is emerging in some of the richer industrial countries may represent a qualitative difference to the past in that it involves the crumbling and instability of the nuclear family (which has itself only relatively recently parted company from the wider extended family). Sorensen makes the point that there are really two types of post-nuclear family arrangement: one is supported by a web of family policies which reduce the economic risks associated with it whereas the other exists without any such support. She describes the first as emerging by choice whereas the second is by misery. In times when the nuclear family is becoming less widespread, the poverty rate depends strongly on the role played by the state. If the family is left to its own devices, as in the USA, then it has a high chance of failing in the poverty stakes. However, if the family is required to play only a minor role in protecting people from poverty, as in Sweden, then poverty is much less likely. As Sorensen (1999, pp.71-72) points out, the Scandinavian countries demonstrate very clearly that it is possible to create decent living conditions for children even in the presence of high marital instability and high rates of single parenthood.

5.3 Fertility

With fertility rates falling across Europe, policy makers' attention has turned to the implications of policies for family size. The relationship between fertility and public policy has also sparked the interest of researchers. This relationship has been explored in terms of both family size and the timing of births.

Studies on the impact of family policies on fertility behaviour rely extensively on the economic theory of fertility. According to this theory, the demand for children is a function of both individual preferences and the costs of children. It therefore predicts that policy measures aimed at reducing such costs will have a positive impact on fertility. The concept of 'costs of children' usually makes a distinction between the direct costs (direct expenditure) and opportunity costs (families' foregone earnings). Policy measures aimed at reducing the former typically include child benefits and other family allowances (such as birth grants) and fiscal measures such as tax allowances for families with children. Measures aimed at reducing the opportunity costs include maternity benefits, parental leave and public childcare provision. Following this theory, the effectiveness of a particular measure in reducing the cost of children will depend on variables such as income replacement rates (higher rates will have stronger effects in reducing opportunity costs) and duration of leave (longer leaves may degrade human capital). Similarly, in the case of other family allowances, such as child benefit, the impact will depend on factors such as size of payment for each child.

If total birth rates and family policies in the five countries under study are compared, no regular pattern can be observed (Table 7). Thus Sweden, the country with the most generous policy package in helping parents to reconcile work and family life, has a lower fertility rate than other countries with less generous packages. In addition, Ireland has the highest fertility rate in Europe and yet it is one of the least generous providers of services. Likewise, although France does more than the UK to help parents reconcile work and family life and offers significantly more generous cash transfers for families with three and more children, the fertility rates in both countries are very similar. The results of research mirror this sense of an inconclusive relationship between fertility and public policy. It must be said, however, that this relationship is a particularly difficult one to frame for research purposes. Issues of method and data are involved.[84] As Hoem (1992, p. 6) points out, causality is obscured when rights and benefits expand gradually and in line with other developments.

Table 7: Total Fertility Rates in Ireland, UK, Sweden, France and Germany (1989-1998)

	1989	1990	1991	1992	1993	1994	1995	1996	1997	1998
Ire.	2.09	2.11	2.08	1.99	1.90	1.85	1.84	1.88	1.92	1.93
UK	1.79	1.83	1.81	1.79	1.75	1.74	1.71	1.72	1.72	1.72
Sw.	2.01	2.13	2.11	2.09	1.99	1.88	1.73	1.60	1.52	1.51
Fr.	1.79	1.78	1.77	1.73	1.65	1.66	1.70	1.72	1.71	1.75
Ger.	1.42	1.45	1.33	1.30	1.28	1.24	1.25	1.32	1.37	1.34

Source: Eurostat (2000).

Gauthier and Hatzius (1997) carried out an empirical analysis of total fertility rates in the context of provision for the family in twenty-two industrialised countries in the period between 1970 and 1990. The family benefits considered in their study were divided into two categories: cash benefits (child benefits) and maternity benefits (paid maternity leave). The study controlled for other determinants of fertility by introducing a set of independent variables related to economic opportunities, such as men and women's average hourly wages and unemployment rates (education was excluded due to a lack of reliable data). Child benefits were found to have a positive link with fertility. The effect was, however, of a limited magnitude: a 25 per cent increase in the value of child benefits would result in a fertility level that is about 0.6 per cent higher in the short-run and 4 per cent higher in the long-run. The magnitude of the effect was found to vary across countries. In particular, there was no evidence to suggest that the available cash benefits affect fertility in the Anglo-Saxon countries although the policy package was found to have a large and consistent effect in the Scandinavian countries, with continental and southern European countries in between these two extremes. In the authors' interpretation, this highlights the generosity of benefits as a factor as well as the more general package of cash and in-kind benefits for families. However maternity leave (either in terms of duration or payment levels) did not appear to be significantly related to fertility.

Hoem (1992) provides a rare demonstration of a direct causal effect of a policy reform on demographic behaviour. Since 1980, women on parental leave in Sweden can retain their eligibility to the benefit from one child to the next if the birth of the new child occurs within a given period of time of the previous birth (twenty-four months up to 1985, thirty months thereafter). In order to assess the impact of this feature on the spacing of children, Hoem looked at the rates of second, third and fourth births for mothers with a youngest child at specific ages over the period 1961-1990. The study found a general increase in second and subsequent birth rates after around 1977. Furthermore, comparing birth rates among mothers with a youngest child aged 24-29 months with those with a youngest child aged 30-35 months revealed a significantly higher birth rate among the first group of mothers after 1985 (when the birth interval for the preservation of eligibility to parental leave rights was extended to 30 months). Before that date, rates for both groups of mothers were very similar. Hoem named the eligibility interval of maternity leave as the 'speed premium.' His work indicates that many Swedish couples are apparently prepared to adjust the timing of their childbearing in order to avail of the economic and practical advantages associated with this measure. Olah's (1998) analysis of the Swedish and Hungarian cases tends to confirm such effects. However the thrust of her findings is to emphasise that a range of public policies is necessary in order to raise fertility. Among these, gender equality has played a big role in Sweden. Thus she found that the chances of second birth are higher when the father took parental leave after the first birth. She sums up her findings on the significance of public policies as follows (1998, pp.35-36):

> Public policies that aim to reduce the conflict between employment and parenthood do facilitate the combination of these competing roles for individuals, especially for women. This, if combined with changes towards more gender equal parenting practices, has a clear positive influence on fertility.

Ronsen (1998, 1999) undertook an analysis of the factors affecting fertility in Norway and Finland, focusing especially on the significance of economic factors, including public policies. Her results underline the complexity of decisions around fertility and generally emphasise that a variety of factors have to be taken into consideration when modelling the fertility process. Among these are the socio-economic status and size of the parental home during adolescence, religiosity, marital status and educational level. In relation to public policies, the study confirms that the economic environment is important for the timing of births. A higher female wage, for example, delays the time of first birth and also reduces the likelihood of a second or third conception. The study also found indications that the extension of maternity leave exerted a positive impact on fertility, especially for higher order births. Judging on the Norwegian experience, better-educated women respond more strongly than other women to the expansion of daycare facilities.

In France, the parental allowance paid during the period of parental leave is only available to qualifying parents who give up (totally or partially) their economic activity in order to care for a second or subsequent child. However, qualifying conditions vary depending on the child's place in the family. While the allowance for a second child is clearly targeted at working mothers (two years of activity within the five years prior to the birth of a child), the parental allowance for the third child is also targeted at mothers who have been outside the labour force for a long time (two years of activity within the previous ten years). There is a decided pronatalist slant to the latter policy. When introduced in 1985 it was subject to strong criticisms by those who saw it as a 'mother's salary' (Jenson and Sineau, 1995). This kind of rationale led many to believe that the allowance may have an impact on fertility and/or on the timing of pregnancies. A study carried out in 1995 – a year and a half after the parental allowance was extended to the second child – pointed to a possible effect of the allowance on the spacing of second births (Afsa, 1996). The study selected one cohort of women who were active in the labour force in 1994 and who had had their second child between July 1994 and June 1995 (before the new policy measure was introduced). Followed up in December 1995, the cohort was divided into two groups, one comprising those women who remained active in the labour force and the other made up of women who had retired from the labour market in order to receive the parental allowance for their second child.[85] The study then compared the average length of interval between first and second births for each group. As expected, these intervals were found to be shorter among the group of women receiving the parental allowance. However, the author was reluctant to draw any definite conclusions from these findings, since she also noted that a high proportion of parental allowance recipients are young women on low incomes, a characteristic generally shared with women who, independently of the allowance, have successive pregnancies close to one another.

Overall there is as yet limited evidence of a relationship between public policy and fertility. The general opinion in the literature seems to be that much work remains to be done on this, very interesting, topic.

5.4 Labour Force Participation of Mothers and Spouses

In contrast to the scarcity of evidence on the relationship between family policies and fertility, a number of studies have shown a significant impact of family policies especially the so-called 'reconciliation policies' (i.e. maternity leave, parental leave, childcare) on the employment of mothers. The relation has generally been found to be positive – employment rates increasing with the level of provision. However, it is important to point out that not all parental leave and childcare policies have the objective of increasing mothers' labour force participation. There is an important analytic distinction to be made between income- or wage-related payments (the principal aim of which is to support mothers' involvement in paid work) and flat-rate payments (which aim to enable mothers to remain in the home as full-time care givers). The latter type of measure is found especially in Germany where, in addition, entitlement to the leave payment is not even linked to labour force participation. This type of unconditional allowance has generally been found to have a negative impact on the labour supply of mothers, as have other policies such as generous child benefits for larger families (as in France) and tax allowances for married couples.

The bulk of research has concentrated on the impact of maternity and parental leave on the one hand and that of childcare provision on the other.

5.4.1 Impact of Paid Maternity and Parental Leave

Table 5 above compared the five countries on their provisions for parental leave. As outlined above, paid maternity and parental leave mandates have been found to have a positive effect on the labour supply of mothers. A recent study of patterns in nine European countries between 1969 and 1993 analysed how extensions of leave affect employment-to-population ratios and hourly wages (Ruhm, 1998). The study found that leave legislation raises the female employment-to-population ratio by between 3 and 4 per cent, with larger effects for women of childbearing age. Ruhm suggests that much of this effect occurs through two processes. In the first instance the leave provides incentives for women to enter employment prior to childbirth (so that they can subsequently qualify for benefits); in the second the leave speeds up the return to work of new mothers. The study also found that short leave entitlements have little effect on women's earnings but that lengthier leave (of say nine months or more) is associated with substantial (2-3 per cent) reductions in relative wages. The latter effect occurs either through the non-wage costs which extended leave imposes on firms or the behavioural effect whereby lengthy leave encourages women to remain out of the labour force for longer. Overall, Ruhm's research indicates that parental leave raises women's employment levels but, at longer durations, may be paid for through the receipt of lower relative wages.

Other research indicates the desirability of taking a longer-term view for a different reason: women's re-entry to employment after childbirth may not be of long duration. One important study in this regard is that of Gustaffson et al (1996) on the impact of parental leave on the employment of mothers. The study compared the labour force transitions of mothers in the UK, Germany and Sweden within the thirty-six months following the birth of their first child. The study found that up to nine months following birth, UK mothers, who are entitled to the shortest maternity leave of the three countries, had the fastest rate of return to employment. However, after nine months, the return rates of Swedish mothers had overtaken those of their UK counterparts. And finally, fifteen months following the birth, UK mothers' return was found to be identical to that of German mothers (who had the longest maximum duration of leave of the three countries), both well below the rate of return of Swedish mothers. These studies also revealed that long extended entitlements, like those available in Finland and Germany, have negative consequences on the labour supply of mothers, since a large proportion of women end up outside the labour force.

Ronsen and Sundstrom's (1999) study compared the impact of parental leave in Finland, Norway and Sweden. The results are quite revealing since each of the three countries had very different parental leave provisions during the period of study. Thus, in the final year of analysis (1992) the maximum leave period in each country was 22 weeks in Norway, 64 weeks in Sweden and 44 weeks in Finland.[86] In general, the study found a much higher overall employment likelihood of entitled mothers compared with non-entitled mothers but no significant differences across countries.

One variable which has been found to be important is mothers' labour force attachment prior to the birth. From country to country this will depend, among other things, on the characteristics of the parental leave regulations such as conditions of entitlement, job protection rights, type and amount of payment, length of leave period, and so forth. Such variation can partly explain, for example, the greater labour market attachment of Swedish leave-takers, as opposed to the poor attachment of their French counterparts. A second factor is the socio-economic context. Thus, as French studies show, in a context of high unemployment and high demand for jobs, parental leave can have a negative impact on the labour market attachment of women with children. In France, a very large proportion of beneficiaries of the parental leave allowance are women who: (a) were unemployed right before the birth of their child or (b) were employed but in a precarious job. This set of characteristics of leave-takers may explain poor employment re-entry rates at the end of the leave period. A recent study (CREDOC, 1999) found that only 55 per cent of women who were employed before the birth of their child had returned to work within three years. The majority of mothers who had held a precarious job before taking the parental allowance were either outside the labour market (30 per cent) or else unemployed (25 per cent). The study also found that the vast majority (93 per cent) of those who returned to the same job were women who had had a stable job before taking up the paid leave and most had benefited from parental leave during the period of payment (which guarantees job protection).

What about the effects of childcare?

5.4.2 Impact of Childcare Provision on Mothers' Employment

There is a large body of empirical research supporting the prediction (based on labour supply theory) that improvements in childcare options will be associated with increases in female employment. A study carried out by Gornick, Meyers and Ross (1997) examined the difference between the employment of mothers with young children and the employment of otherwise similar mothers whose children are older. The difference they name as the 'child penalty'. According to the authors, the advantage of using this measure is that it helps to isolate the impact of government policy on women's employment outcomes from other demographic, economic, and cultural factors. The countries with the highest level of childcare provision in Europe (France and Sweden) were found to have no 'child penalties' while the most substantial child penalties were found in the UK, one of the countries with the lowest level of provision. The authors conclude that, although several alternative explanations for the association between public policies supporting the employment of mothers (such as childcare) and mothers' labour supply could be offered, a strong case exists for the argument that these policies influence employment. The study generally confirms the predictions, grounded in economic theory, that an improvement in public provision of childcare will have an impact on the employment of mothers.

The work of Joshi and Davies (1992) is one of the few studies to focus on opportunity costs for women associated with the availability or not of childcare. Their work is helpful in drawing attention to the fact that such costs should be seen in relative rather than absolute terms – not just whether the mother works at all but rather how many hours does or can she work and what is the relative loss or gain in wages. Their results and those of others indicate that the effects of public policies will vary with the number of children in the family and the age of the children, especially the youngest. Ireland is among the countries where the number of children matters and is joined by France, the USA and the Mediterranean nations. Comparative research indicates that the age of the youngest child matters more to women's employment in countries where childcare is not subsidised and its availability is limited (Dex and Joshi, 1999). Comparing the opportunity costs of children in four countries, Joshi and Davies find that these costs are highest in the UK and Germany where the availability of public support forces mothers either to remain out of the labour market for longer when they have a child or to be employed on a part-time basis. The costs are much lower for Swedish mothers and to the extent that they exist are occasioned by their reducing their hours of work. French mothers suffer the lowest opportunity costs, an effect which the authors attribute to the greater availability in that country of childcare facilities and the longer school day.

Daly (2000) attempts an overview. Her work looks at the impact of the two sets of measures across a large number of countries and shows that the orientation of the policy package is quite closely related to mothers' employment behaviour. This is to be seen especially in how country groupings distinguish themselves from one another, although there are discrepant relationships or placings for a number of countries and one must be careful about assuming causality in this regard because several factors are involved. Judging from the experience of Scandinavia, it appears that when the policy package offers women a high degree of choice they choose to be in the labour market. It is important to note, though, that in Sweden more than half of all employed mothers are employed only on a part-time basis. Looking at other countries, medium levels of public support for maternal employment also appear to have the desired effect. These countries are not always consistent in their approach to maternal employment but they tend to opt for a set of policies that enable (or entice) mothers to be out of the labour force through relatively generous sets of leaves and so on. In Germany and the Netherlands, moderate levels of provision are associated with moderate levels of maternal employment. A considerable proportion of these employed mothers work on a part-time basis and in the Netherlands 90 per cent are part-time. Low levels of choice are also associated with the expected pattern of maternal employment. However, at least part of the constraint on mothers' employment in Greece, Ireland, Italy, Luxembourg and Spain is the general low availability of part-time employment. The UK, the USA and Canada are exceptional cases. In these nations mothers' labour force participation is either high or moderate despite a low degree of support from public policies. These might not be as exceptional as they seem, for when they are put together with the other cases the following general explanation of the relation between maternal employment and public policy suggests itself. The employment of mothers depends primarily on the availability of childcare facilities. These can be and sometimes are provided free of charge or subsidised by public facilities (as in Scandinavia). Alternatively they can be provided by low-cost private facilities. The existence of the latter is, however, contingent on low wages and low non-wage labour costs. This is essentially the liberal model. In the continental European nations, the provision of public facilities is limited but low wage differentials and high non-wage labour costs increase the price of childcare. Hence labour force participation on the part of mothers in these countries is on the low side.

Overall it is important to point out that mothers' employment rates cannot be seen solely as a function of public policy treatment of families with children. They are shaped by a more complex mix, drawing also upon market factors such as the size and nature of the service sector, wage rates and differentials and non-wage costs. In any case, child-related policies have many objectives and are better understood as being about balancing a series of aims rather than solely about facilitating maternal employment. The reconciliation of work and family life typically sits alongside other concerns such as the education and welfare of children, the wellbeing of families and the balancing of public and private responsibilities more generally. With such a broad range of objectives, the room for ambiguity, contradictions and perverse effects is large. In the event, family policy in general and policies oriented to the care of children in particular, are nowhere unambiguously interpretable as having the support of maternal employment as their primary objective. There is, therefore, no unidimensional interpretation of these and other policy domains and it is important not to generalise too readily from the Scandinavian model.

Chapter 6

Challenging Issues in Relation to the Family for Policy in Ireland

One of the central objectives of this research is to identify policy issues for Ireland on the basis of current trends, existing policy provisions and recent developments in Ireland and other countries. This chapter addresses that objective. It will identify and examine some of the larger issues pertaining to provision for the family in Ireland and reflect upon these on the basis of experience in other countries. The chapter is divided into two parts. The first identifies outstanding issues on the basis of matters which have been the subject of policy review and popular debate in Ireland. Discussion and review is in itself an innovation in the Irish social policy scene, which has not often found itself the subject of popular debate and discourse. This is part of a wider change in the approach to (social) policy making in Ireland whereby new initiatives tend to be more strategic and to be preceded by fairly thorough reviews. Hence the 1990s witnessed a plethora of both internal and external reviews of a range of family-related policy matters, including a major review of the state of the family itself. These reviews have served a number of functions. From the social researcher's perspective they act to reveal what are regarded as being the key issues for policy as well as showing how these issues are framed and resolutions to them sought. Looking at them from the first perspective, the principles of family policy, the matter of individualisation, childcare and the rights of children and provision for lone parents and carers are among the most pressing issues. It must also be said, however, that many of these reviews have been inconclusive. Some issues which reviews were set up to consider, or which they encountered and raised in the course of their deliberations, remain outstanding. The fact that they are inconclusive serves to underline the complexity of the issues involved. They touch on matters that go to the core of Irish society. The second part of the chapter will revisit these issues and reflect upon them and other matters in the light of developments and experience elsewhere.

6.1 Debates Relevant to Family Policy in the Last Decade

While the 1990s was a very active decade in terms of both discourse and policy action, four main issues dominated the family policy agenda (broadly conceived). These include the principles of family policy, matters relating to individualisation of benefits, childcare, and the situation of lone parents. The main points of these debates will now be briefly outlined.

6.1.1 Principles of Family Policy

The Commission on the Family undertook not just to review provision but to work out a set of principles for Irish policy on the family. The philosophical principles which it set out for family policy relate to: (a) the functions of the family (to provide care and nurture for its members), (b) the place of the family in society (a fundamental unit for stability and wellbeing, membership of which confers rights, duties and responsibilities), and (c) the nature of family relationships (requiring stability and continuity). Given this interpretation of the family and its needs, policy must recognise an equality of wellbeing among family members and a diversity of family forms and relationships. The priority attached by the Commission to equality matters within the family is very significant in an Irish context where policy in the past has tended either to take the family as a unit or to treat people at one remove from their family situation.

Taking an integrated and holistic approach to the family, the Commission directed its activities to four 'desirable outcomes':

• building strengths in families;

• supporting families in carrying out their functions;

• promoting continuity and stability in family life;

• protecting and enhancing the position of children and vulnerable dependent family members.

The first issue is defined mainly in terms of disadvantaged families (although there is no analysis of the problems which these families might be experiencing) and the response for the most part consists of the establishment of a network of family and community resource centres (to provide a range of support and training activities) and, on the part of the social welfare system, a more customised, integrated and family-oriented service. A service-oriented response also predominates in regard to the second objective – supporting families to carry out their functions. This includes support with educational programmes for parents in general and for lone parents, together with measures to facilitate employment with family caregiving and greater recognition in employment and social policies of the caring work carried out by parents. A significant gap is identified in services for pre-school children and the Commission took the position that the state has a role in providing financial support to meet the needs of such children (whether they are being cared for at home or elsewhere). The Commission's failure to recommend a particular method of financial support to assist with the care of young children is however notable. It left a gap where policy makers needed direction. In regard to the third desired outcome – promoting stability and continuity in family life – the Commission called for support of marriage in public policies, the availability of accessible services to promote and maintain stable relations and, in the event of marital breakdown, services to assist families to make the transition. Counselling, mediation and relationship services loom large as responses here. In relation to the final desired outcome – to recognise and cater for the varied needs of children and the contribution and welfare of the elderly – a service-related response also dominates. It is important to note, though, that little or no provider role for the state is envisaged. Rather, the appropriate activity on the part of the state is to co-ordinate developments and direct assistance for the development of services which are run and operated by others.

The analysis, conclusions and recommendations of the Commission on the Family were comprehensive but not radical in the sense that they did not envision a change in the status quo. In comparison to say the National Children's Strategy, the Commission remained within the traditional model of social policy in Ireland. A problematic aspect of its approach was its failure to strike sufficient balance between supporting marriage and the family form based on it and supporting diversity in family life. One could argue that it favoured the former. This links into a particular way of thinking, quite common in policy circles around the family in Ireland and elsewhere, which aims to get policy to restabilise the family (Smart, 1997, p. 303). Even though there is an acknowledgement that things are changing, the dominant framework is to get back to a specific and knowable family form. This appears to be the Commission's underlying position.

6.1.2 Issues Relating to Individualisation

Some 80,000 people receive social welfare as the adult 'dependant' of another claimant. While this situation might have been acceptable in the past, it is something of an anomaly in an age when people are more and more expected to be economically self-sufficient. For a country like Ireland which has tended to hold to a strong male breadwinner model of social provision, issues of individualisation are bound to be contentious. They have been on the agenda for a considerable time and have been the subject of more than one review.

Individualisation is in fact quite a complex term. In discussions about it, the term may be used in two ways. The first refers to the individualisation of social security rights. This notion of individualisation is used in contrast to the notion of derived rights – rights that are acquired by virtue of marriage or a relationship to another member of one's household. For this purpose a differentiation is made between the holder of direct and indirect rights (with the former denoted as a 'qualified adult'). The individualisation of social security rights implies the abolition, or at least the limitation, of derived rights and the development of direct rights. The second usage of individualisation refers to individualisation of the basis of entitlement. The reference here is to individualisation in contrast to the aggregation of the means and incomes of more than one person. Such aggregation has most commonly taken the form of assessment of couples and their children for means-tested benefits and/or personal income taxation (McLaughlin, 1999).

In Ireland, the issue of individualisation has attracted attention for a variety of reasons and in a variety of contexts. The following are the main ways in which it has been discussed:

- as a measure to eliminate elements of fiscal and social protection policies which discourage women's participation in the formal labour market: The disincentive effects of the system of qualified adult allowances on the labour force participation of women have been raised in a number of reports, including that of the Expert Working Group on the Integration of the Tax and Social Welfare Systems (1996). The report of the conference 'Beyond Equal Treatment – Social Security in a Changing Europe' (held in Dublin in 1996) concluded that male bread-winner-oriented social security systems have a negative impact on female labour supply and proposed as a solution to make social security contributions independent of employment situation. This is a recurrent theme in EU policy as well.

- as a measure to eliminate elements of fiscal and social protection policies which discourage marriage, cohabitation and joint parenting: This was a theme raised in the Final Report of the Commission on the Family (1998) and the Review of the One-Parent Family Payment (2000).

- as a measure to eliminate inequality among different households: It is in this context that the examination of individualisation in the Report of the Working Group Examining the Treatment of Married, Cohabiting and One-Parent Families under the Tax and Social Welfare Codes (1999) should be viewed.
- as a measure aimed at combating poverty and social exclusion: The role of individualisation as a measure to fight the gender dimension of poverty was raised in the 1997 National Anti-Poverty Strategy.

The most recent examination of the issue of individualisation was carried out by the working group Examining the Treatment of Married, Cohabiting and One-Parent Families under the Tax and Social Welfare Codes which reported in 1999. One of the objectives of this Working Group was to identify and cost ways of ensuring consistent and equitable treatment of household types under the tax and social welfare codes. An examination of the issue of individualisation was considered relevant by virtue of its potential to diminish and eradicate differences in the treatment of different household types.

Five possible approaches to individualisation were examined by the Working Group, namely:

1. total independent treatment in the social welfare system so that each individual is able to claim a payment in his/her own right, based on either his/her contribution record or own income;
2. expansion of the social insurance system so as to replace derived rights with direct participatory rights;
3. individualisation of the resources allocated to spouses and partners working in the home. This option, presented by McCashin in his (1999) paper on reforming the tax/welfare treatment of households, would involve the abolition of payments for qualified adults and tax allowances for spouses and the introduction of a Home Responsibility Allowance payable to housewives or homemakers. The latter could be targeted only at couples with children;

4. administrative individualisation whereby the same amounts as in the current social welfare system would be paid on a split basis between the couple;[87]
5. assessment for means-tested social welfare payments on a couple basis but once entitlement is established payment of full rates on an individual basis. This is a variant of the fourth option.

One of the fundamental principles adopted by the Working Group was that of horizontal equity, namely that all persons or groups in the same situation or circumstances should be treated equitably insofar as entitlement to payment is concerned. Of the approaches to individualisation examined, the first and second options best satisfy this principle since they rely on the concept of citizenship and individual rights, as opposed to the current system wherein many payments (particularly social assistance payments) are based on the notion of derived rights. However, the different approaches to individualisation were also evaluated against other principles adopted by the Working Group. These included:

- adequacy (according to which future changes to the tax and social welfare codes should be made on the principle that the circumstances of families most at risk and their chances of moving out of poverty are not worsened and are if possible improved);
- positive labour/behavioural incentives (whereby the tax and social welfare systems should provide incentives for people to make the transition from social welfare to work);
- consistency in the treatment of individuals and households under both the tax and social welfare systems;
- affordability.

Although the Working Group did not reach agreement on total independent treatment, there was general agreement about extending the administrative arrangements in the area of separate payments and also that individualisation in the social welfare code should take place via the social insurance system. The first option – total independent treatment in the social welfare system – was generally considered to be very costly.

6.1.3 Issues Relating to Childcare

This is an important and potentially divisive issue in Ireland. It is also one which government has difficulty in addressing, especially on the demand side. A number of policy reviews have considered it, including the Final Report of the Commission on the Family (1998), the Report of the Expert Working Group on the Integration of the Tax and Social Welfare Systems (1996), the Report of the Working Group Examining the Treatment of Married, Cohabiting and One-Parent Families under the Tax and Social Welfare Codes (1999) and the National Childcare Strategy (Expert Working Group on Childcare, 1999). The dilemma around childcare seems to centre around a choice between vertical and horizontal equity. Two main alternatives to current policy have been suggested:

- introducing a special rate of child benefit for children under three years;
- integrating child benefit with taxation.

Both the Commission on the Family and the Working Group Examining the Treatment of Married, Cohabiting and One-Parent Families under the Tax and Social Welfare Codes examined the first option. It was seen to have powerful advantages. For example the Commission on the Family pointed out that a special rate of child benefit for children aged under three years:

- presents neither incentives nor disincentives for mothers' participation in the labour market;
- is neutral as to the choices parents make in relation to the care of their children;
- could provide the basis for progress towards a basic income for children in the youngest age group.

The Working Group Examining the Treatment of Married, Cohabiting and One-Parent Families under the Tax and Social Welfare Codes proposed that increased child benefit for children aged under three years could be financed by revenue raised from placing restrictions on the transferability of tax allowances and/or rate bands between partners in couples.

The report of the Expert Working Group on the Integration of the Tax and Social Welfare Systems (1996), conscious of significant employment disincentives and poverty traps in the existing system of child income support, considered reforming it through the introduction of what they call an 'integrated child benefit'. This would involve increasing the level of child benefit and making it eligible for taxation, thereby reducing the total cost by clawing back a proportion of the payment from taxpayers. This accords priority to vertical redistribution (redistribution across income groups) over considerations of horizontal equity (redistribution from people without children to those with children) because the higher income earners get less. Since 1990, the National Economic and Social Council has consistently argued for this option as the best one available from an anti-poverty perspective, although in its report (1999) it acknowledges the difficulties of reconciling childcare and child poverty objectives in relation to the taxation of child benefit.

The fact that the objectives of childcare are so diverse, each dictating certain priority considerations in formulating future policy, poses a challenge to policy makers. It is by no means a simple matter to design a policy package that meets all objectives in a balanced way. There appear to be three objectives or principles underlying the Irish debate. The difficulty of aligning, or prioritising, them is immense.

Principle 1 The first principle is that policy measures to support parents with the costs of childcare should give them a genuine choice as regards the preferred type of childcare arrangement. This consideration received particular emphasis in the Final Report of the Commission on the Family. According to the Commission, future policy should provide direct support to parents when their childcare responsibilities are at their most demanding and facilitate their taking time out of the workforce if this is their preferred way of caring for their young children. With this as the guiding framework, a support package comprising measures benefiting only employed parents (e.g. an improved Family Income Supplement) would have to be rejected on the grounds that it would be of no use to 'full-time parents'. The Commission put forward three possible demand-side options:

- parent allowance and childcare allowance;
- extended paid parental leave;
- increased child benefit for children under the age of three.

It failed to recommend one over another.

Principle 2 The second principle is that support should be equitable and so should be provided to parents regardless of their income and employment status. According to this principle, if tax relief measures are introduced, they should be complemented by other measures aimed at families (including those with unemployed members) which, because of their low incomes, are outside the tax net. This point received particular emphasis in the National Economic and Social Council's 1999 report *Opportunities, Challenges and Capacities for Choice.* Similarly, the Commission on the Family did not view tax relief as the most suitable mechanism for the provision of support for families with this aspect of their child-rearing responsibilities, since it would be of no value to low-income families and would not be of direct benefit to those working full-time in the home.

Principle 3 The third principle is that measures supporting demand should also encourage supply. According to the report of the 1999 Expert Working Group on Childcare (The National Childcare Strategy), supply and demand are interconnected and so measures for each need to be implemented as a package in order to be successful. Therefore, demand-side measures which do not guarantee an increase in the provision of childcare places would be rejected unless they are accompanied by investment to improve the quality and quantity of supply. On these grounds, and also on the basis of costs, the Expert Working Group did not recommend an increased child benefit as a suitable solution. The group opted instead for a diversified approach, making the following recommendations with respect to demand-side measures:

- childcare subsidies;
- improvements to the Family Income Supplement;
- increased ceilings for the One-Parent Family Payment;
- personal tax relief;
- cessation of the treatment of childcare as benefit-in-kind.

In its 1999 report, the NESC expressed agreement with the Expert Working Group in favouring the introduction of a programme of suitable measures on both the demand and supply sides rather than one or two isolated proposals. However, (unlike the Expert Group) the National Economic and Social Council favoured an increased child benefit which would be liable for tax as part of the policy response to the demand-side issue. The Council did, however, recognise that the gross value of child benefit would have to be increased substantially for its after-tax value to make a meaningful contribution to childcare costs.

It seems, then, that a range of different measures are required to satisfactorily provide for childcare.

6.1.4 Issues Relating to Lone Parents

Debate on lone-parent families has centred on two issues: the extent to which public policy should encourage or compel them to be employed; matters of maintenance and support. Debate, discussion and review have taken place against a background whereby spending on the One-Parent Family Payment has been growing by about 15 per cent a year.

The Final Report of the Commission on the Family, while supporting an employment-led policy for lone-parent families, was of the view that such a policy should not undermine the core objective of the One-Parent Family Payment which is to provide secure income support for lone parents caring for their children.[88] This view is in line with the philosophy of the Commission which holds that parents are the primary carers and educators of their children and that policy should facilitate and support parents in the choices they make in relation to the care of their children. However, the Working Group Examining the Treatment of Married, Cohabiting and One-Parent Families under the Tax and Social Welfare Codes raised the issue of whether participation in the labour force should be a matter of choice for lone parents. According to the Working Group, the fact that there is no work requirement and/or time limit attached to the social welfare payment for lone parents may be affecting not only the labour force participation of lone parents but also the formation of stable relationships. The Group put forward the option of changing the nature of the One-Parent Family Payment to a short- or medium-term payment which would continue to be paid until the youngest child was five years of age.

Matters relating to the employment of lone parents were examined in more detail by the Department of Social, Community and Family Affairs in its Review of the One-Parent Family Payment (2000). While recognising that this benefit can create undesirable conditions of dependency on social welfare, the Review Group seemed to be of the view that social security provisions in Ireland are unlikely to be acting to trap lone-parent recipients in part-time, low-paid employment since earnings are not concentrated just below threshold levels (Department of Social, Community and Family Affairs, 2000, p.79). The Review Group failed to reach agreement as to how the matter of the employment or not of lone-parent beneficiaries should be addressed. Some members supported improvements on existing features of the scheme whereas others favoured a compulsory test or time limit on entitlement. Overall, the Review Group concluded that, although reform of the One-Parent Family Payment as a long-term payment might be one of the changes considered in the future, any developments in relation to the issue of compulsory work tests or time limits should not be implemented at this juncture because of the lack of childcare infrastructure as well as a lack of popular support.[89] One could conclude, therefore, that the thrust of policy in Ireland is to permit the Irish lone parent to raise her or his family's total income above the benefit level without jeopardising either the benefit or commitment to the care of her or his children. However, employment and employability are not ruled out. Both the Review Group and the Commission on the Family proposed a more pro-active policy for recipients of the One-Parent Family Payment in relation to employment, training and education (something akin to the New Deal for Lone Parents in the UK).[90]

The second issue relevant to lone parents which has generated some debate is the matter of maintenance. In its Final Report, the Commission on the Family expressed concern that the tax and social welfare system may be putting obstacles in the way of joint parenting and joint responsibility for children. Two factors were identified as possible obstacles:

• the more generous earnings disregards for the One-Parent Family Payment as compared with other social assistance payments;
• the cohabitation rule which leads to the payment being withdrawn in cases of cohabitation or joint custody.

The issue of the likely disincentive effects associated with existing policy was also considered by the Working Group Examining the Treatment of Married, Cohabiting and One-Parent Families under the Tax and Social Welfare Codes. This report showed how a couple with a child considering marriage or cohabitation may experience income losses as high as nearly €127 a week.[91] The Group concluded that, although individualisation would deal with some of the reasons causing the losses (i.e. economies of scale and household means test), it would not deal with the losses associated with a change of status of the lone parent. In order to address this problem, the Group considered that a change in the nature of the One-Parent Family Payment was needed and proposed the introduction of a 'work-test'. However, no agreement on the issue was reached.

The Commission on the Family highlighted a somewhat different type of disincentive – how offsetting maintenance payments against the One-Parent Family Payment (except for the €95 housing disregard) is acting as a disincentive for fathers/parents to pay maintenance. On this issue, the Commission recommended that mechanisms be developed to ensure that partners have an incentive to pay. The Review of the One-Parent Family Payment followed up on this concern by examining two ways of providing incentives to encourage the payment of maintenance:

* a flat weekly disregard;
* allowing the recipient of the One-Parent Family Payment to retain half of any maintenance received.

Upon examination, it considered the second option the better approach, since the first may have the undesirable effect of making parents restrict their contributions to within the specified limit. Both the Commission on the Family and the Review Group were of the view that the Family Mediation Service (which in 1998 was transferred to the Department of Social, Community and Family Affairs from the Department of Justice, Equality and Law Reform and has been recently expanded nation-wide) is of relevance in relation to the policy objective of enhancing lone parents access to maintenance.

6.2 Outstanding Issues

Given that no consensus was reached by the majority of the review exercises, we have to treat individualisation, childcare and the appropriate manner of support for lone parents as issues which remain to be resolved in family policy in Ireland. Not all of these are equally pressing. It appears that there is a general consensus around existing provisions for lone parents. The review of the One-Parent Family Payment seemed to indicate a general satisfaction with existing provision. The issues of individualisation and how the state should support the care of children are more contentious. They should not however be seen in isolation.

Issues such as these should be framed and discussed in the broadest possible terms, not because a broad discussion per se is to be valued but rather because issues are contentious when they touch upon deep-rooted social patterns and conflicting sets of interests. In other words, they affect and are in turn affected by a series of larger balances in society. When one takes a broad view of the unresolved issues in Irish family policy and places them in an international perspective, they can be organised in terms of four broad headings: care, the desired model of family, equity issues, and the relationship between benefits and the labour market. The remainder of this chapter discusses these issues. It need hardly be pointed out that they are themselves inter-related and that they are separated out only for the purposes of discussion.

6.2.1 Care

Ireland lacks a worked-out policy on care. Defining care in an inclusive way to refer to the activities and relations involved in taking care of children, the elderly, ill and disabled adults, is a complex good for policy formulation purposes. Given this, it is helpful to set out a number of benchmarks for the purposes of a comprehensive policy on care.

A first dimension of complexity arises from the fact that making provision for care may entail the satisfaction of three needs: a need for services, for time, and for financial support. In this context it is interesting to observe that Irish social policy tends to respond to care in unidimensional and partial terms. Where the state has responded, cash payments (for care of the elderly) and cash incentives and some time off (in the case of childcare) have been the dominant response. In some respects the problems around childcare in Ireland may be interpreted as a difficulty in moving from a unidimensional to a multi-dimensional perspective or response. Ireland is not alone in this general difficulty. What the international experience suggests, though, is that in times like the present where diversity in life choices is highly valued, a multi-dimensional response around care is vital.

A second complicating aspect of care is that as a policy good it has two components: the person experiencing the set of needs that comprise care and the actor who seeks or is assigned to satisfy that need. This also has implications for policy and again shows the Irish policy response in a different light. For example, it has generally been assumed by policy in Ireland (and indeed also elsewhere) that to make provision for one side of the caring process (either provider or receiver) is to automatically provide for the needs of the other. This is not the case. The implications of a dual view are far-reaching: they suggest, for example, that childcare should be conceived of in terms of the needs of the person providing the care (parent or paid provider) as well as those of the receiver (the child). Again, policy is rarely framed in this way. One important lesson to be learnt from the experience of other countries is that choice should be an important policy objective. This means, for example, that policy should ensure that family members have a choice about whether they personally want to provide the care or not (in the case of both the elderly and children) just as the receiver of care should have a choice about from whom, where and how the care is provided.

Thirdly, given that care is so diversified – involving physical, social and emotional elements – it crosses a number of policy boundaries. These include social policy, employment policy, fiscal policy, health and education policy. Again the Irish response needs to be fleshed out within and across policy domains but it appears rather one-dimensional in terms of policy domains (in that it is mainly consigned to social policy). Because care is such a broad-ranging policy good, there is of course the danger of fragmentation. Policy makers must be on their guard against this. Taking an overview, the possible policy interventions range through cash payments, taxation allowances, different types of paid and unpaid leave, social security credits, services and incentives towards employment creation in the provision of care. Figure 2, summarising the measures that are to be found across Europe as a whole, gives an idea of the options that are available. While no European country has

Figure 2: *Universe of Provision for Care in European Countries*

Type of measure	Social*	Labour Market	Education	Health#	Income
Cash payments	means-tested or social insurance benefits paid to carer or care receiver; childcare vouchers	severance pay for withdrawal for reasons of parent-motherhood		subsidies/ subventions for residential care	
Credits for social security	credits to carers for pension and other social security benefits				
Taxation					allowances for care-related expenses
Leave	paid and unpaid parental, paternity and care leaves	career breaks, time savings account, employment rights during leave	educational/ training leave for caring		
Services	public childcare, home helps, meals on wheels	workplace childcare	Crèches, day care, schools, kindergarten	residential services	
Incentives towards employment creation	vouchers for domestic employment, exemptions from social security contributions for people employed as carers	reduction of working time, part-time working			tax reductions on the costs of employing domestic helpers
Incentives for market services	subsidies towards costs of care in private provision				tax allowances for the cost of care in market-run services

* Services that fall under this heading may actually be offered by the local authorities/communes.

\# Provisions by the housing authorities may also be pertinent here.

the whole palette of measures in place, the lesson of care provision over the last thirty years or so appears to be that the more diversified the policy measures the better. However, such diversification notwithstanding, publicly-provided services play a key role.

It is helpful at this stage to summarise developments in care across Europe. Little recent work has been done on this in relation to the elderly but, according to Rostgaard and Fridberg (1998, p. 36), care policies for older people in Europe today mainly aim to provide in-home services to allow older people to remain in their own home, postponing institutional care for as long as possible. Many countries are also placing special attention on the needs of carers.

Schippers, Siegers and de Jong-Gierveld (1998, p.191) identify the following developments in relation to childcare across Europe:

- there is a search for greater diversity and flexibility in regard to: (a) services themselves in expanding the range of needs they meet (especially the needs of non-employed parents) (Belgium, Denmark, Finland, France, Germany, Italy, Luxembourg, Spain), and (b) the providers of services especially by encouraging private providers to make a greater contribution to publicly-provided services (Finland, Sweden, UK);
- greater efforts are made to encourage more parental involvement in parent-run services (Austria, Denmark, France, Germany);
- improved training is offered for centre-based workers and family day carers (Belgium, Denmark, Finland, France, Germany, Ireland, Italy, Portugal, Spain, Sweden, UK);
- there are changes in the starting age and hours of compulsory schooling (Finland, Greece, Italy, Luxembourg, Sweden, UK);
- there is an evolving relationship between schools and services providing care and recreation for school-aged children (Belgium, Denmark, Sweden);
- actual or proposed changes are being made in the regulation of private services either to make regulation tighter (Ireland, UK) or looser (Germany, Netherlands);

- there is an expansion or development of subsidies made directly to parents to reduce the costs of using services (Denmark, France, Spain, UK).

6.2.2 Family and Gender-related Issues

Individualisation is as we have seen both a contentious and unresolved issue in Ireland. It too hinges on a larger set of discussions. We believe that individualisation is best viewed within the rubric of general models of family life which in turn involves particular household patterns of procuring both care and employment. Obviously, particular roles for women and men, and particular interpretations of gender equality and of the meaning of reconciliation of work and home (paid and unpaid work), are involved as well. There is a choice of family models available. Adapting the work of Threlfall (2000), it is helpful to focus on four such models. These are reproduced in Figure 3 with particular emphasis on the reconciliation of work and family life as a policy instrument. Note that in this regard reconciliation policies are assumed to involve both time and money and therefore have implications for the reorganisation of working time as well as for income support and tax policies. Note further that we assume in all of these models that the old breadwinner model, especially as it involved unpaid caring, is gone. We believe this to be true even for Ireland – we interpret the debates about and (the admittedly still fledgling) provision for childcare as evidence that we have in this country moved to a new level in the relationship between the family and the state.

The first model resembles the traditional breadwinner model but is actually quite different from it in that it presumes that the full-time carer will receive recompense from the state for the work involved in caring. Their unpaid work is therefore transformed into paid work. The main weakness of this model is that it involves no change in the status quo, especially in that the full-time earner undertakes no greater involvement in family life. It therefore institutionalises the traditional division of labour instead of helping to erode it. In the second model, the carer becomes a part-time worker/carer, thereby supplementing the family income and making for a certain degree of continuity in the provision of care. Public policy in this model must facilitate the creation and legitimisation (for social security and other purposes) of part-time jobs, ensure the supply of the necessary caring services and compensate the half-time carer/earner with both time and money (on a half-time basis). This model shares the disadvantage of the first in that no reconciliation is required of or for the main earner. It therefore runs the risk of the carer moving simply from being unpaid to being low paid. The third option is the two breadwinner model. In this model both parents work full-time and there is no time reconciliation for family life. Extensive care services are needed and the care needs of children and other relatives are largely dealt with by others. Finally, there is the double half-carer, half-provider model. This is, according to Threlfall (2000, pp. 194-5), the 'ideal' model of reconciling family life and paid work because both parents share employment and care work. It must be said, however, that this model requires considerable financial

Figure 3: Models of Full or Partial Reconciliation between Paid Work and Family Life for Both Sexes

Model	Policy architecture
Breadwinner/homemaker (1 full-time employee + 1 full-time carer)	payment from the state for the parent or carer; no 'time' reconciliation for the full-time breadwinner; some care services
One and a half earners (1 full-time earner + 1 half-time earner/carer)	part-time parents/carers' allowance; 'time' reconciliation for the carer; no 'time' reconciliation for the full-time breadwinner
Two breadwinners (2 full-time earners)	'pay' reconciliation for both; no 'time' reconciliation for either; widespread care services
The double half-carer, half provider (2 half-time earners + 2 half-time carers)	'pay' reconciliation for both; 'time' reconciliation for both; some care services

recompense from public funds for parents because so much part-time work is low paid. The model depends for its viability also on the spread of part-time and flexible working hours, job-sharing and other arrangements to promote flexibility. It is especially premised on the willingness (and capacity) of fathers to reduce their hours of paid work in favour of caring work. This last model is probably the least developed in Europe – though the 'combination scenario' in the Netherlands comes rather close to it. This is a model wherein women and men participate in both paid labour and unpaid care tasks (Brouwer and Wierda, 1998). This model is interesting not least because, as well as considering the division of care between women and men, it also takes into account where households are to 'source' the care. However, it is by and large driven by labour market and economic considerations, rather than those of the quality of family life.

The meaning of fatherhood and motherhood is key in all of this. It is important to point out, along with Threlfall (2000, p. 186), that the reconciliation of paid work and family life is, ultimately, a proposal for men to spend less time at work and more time raising children, looking after sick relatives and performing household chores. Getting men to share in the family has always been a big challenge but it is one that has never been centrally addressed by public policy in Ireland, either in the domain of incomes policy or in other social policy areas. It is something that could be considered by the National Framework Committee for Family Friendly Policies. This Committee, established under the Programme for Prosperity and Fairness, is charged with supporting and facilitating family friendly policies through the development of a package of measures at the level of the firm or enterprise. In regard to the extent to which public policy has addressed the issue and meaning of fatherhood, Ireland is not widely adrift of policy elsewhere in Europe. Only the Scandinavian countries, and especially Norway and Sweden, have adopted this as an explicit social (rather than economic) goal of policy. Indeed they have pursued what amounts almost to a social engineering approach, setting aside a proportion of the parental leave for men and penalising the family (by the loss of the leave) if men do not take their share. It has by all accounts been successful. As one commentator (Cohen, 1999, p. 296) sums up:

> Heavily promoted, monitored and subsequently modified, parental leave in Sweden offers families a meaningful parental care option and has achieved a higher take-up among fathers than in any other member state. Half of all fathers in Sweden now take parental leave for an average of approximately two months.

Ireland appears to be at a different stage. Judging on the basis of the approach taken by the Commission on the Family, for example, which made hardly any specific reference to the role of fathers, Ireland has yet to have the broader discussion about the social role of fathers.[92] This debate is rather urgent at this stage, not least because of the changes taking place in marriage and patterns of parenting and especially the increase in the numbers of separated and single fathers and mothers.

6.2.3 Equity

The debates that are being carried on in this country about such matters as individualisation, childcare and so forth are essentially debates about how the welfare state itself should change. Ireland faces a big decision about the appropriate mix of universalism and selectivity in its social policy model. Decisions about how to subsidise care, for example, go to the heart of the (existing and desirable) policy model. Equity has been a central consideration in the discussions. The question of the relationship between horizontal and vertical equity is still undecided (Combat Poverty Agency, 2000). Horizontal redistribution is synonymous with a conception of the family as the fundamental social unit which the state is bound to protect whereas vertical redistribution emphasises the social dimension of family policies (Letablier and Rieucau, 2000, p. 224). One can, we believe, trace the failure to agree an approach to care and other outstanding issues to indecision in Ireland about equity goals. Ireland shares such indecision with its neighbours, other European countries find it difficult also to decide on which is the more desirable goal or, indeed, how the two should co-exist. However, Ireland has never made a strong commitment to horizontal redistribution. Despite recent increases, provision for children overall in this country is low (Fahey and Fitz Gerald, 1997; Plumb and Walsh, 2000).

It should not be forgotten that childcare and early childhood education are also closely associated with equity. These are in most other countries conceived of as goods for children in contrast to Ireland where childcare is mainly seen as a matter of mothers' participation in the labour market. This is too one-sided. If childcare and early childhood education are seen from the perspective and interests of children, matters of quality and indeed equity are pushed much more to the fore. Equity issues are especially important in regard to service provision. The experience of France in recent years suggests that where governments put their resources into enabling people to purchase or provide services for themselves, a class divide begins to emerge. In other words, universal services are most egalitarian.

As a step towards further clarity, the debate about how to assist families with the costs and exigencies of care might be conducted in terms which distinguish clearly between direct and indirect assistance. As we have seen in Chapter 5, the move in Europe is towards assisting families with the indirect costs of children by subsidising childcare. This is done in one of two ways: either the state provides the services or parents are given subsidies or allowances which are to be spent by them on either purchasing childcare or providing it themselves. The trend in Ireland is different. The strategy pursued thus far has been to upgrade the universal benefits for children and to encourage the private supply of services either through informal provision or commercial provision and that by employers. These are not necessarily incompatible but it is noticeable that we have not been able to come up with an adequate demand-side strategy. It is worth pointing out in this context that social policy classically offered a broad range of supports to families.

6.2.4   *The Relationship between Benefit Receipt and the Labour Market*

The link between benefits and the labour market has always troubled social policy. It is raised in different guises at different points in time. Lately it has appeared in a focus on what are called the 'activation effects of policy', by which is meant the general and specific (in terms of individual behaviour) relationship between social policy and the labour market. Social policies are increasingly scrutinised for their effects in creating dependency on the one hand and in negatively affecting the performance and structure of the labour market on the other. In this kind of climate, attention has turned to the potential of the tax system as an alternative source of support. Current international opinion is emphasising the advantages of tax credits in positively affecting incentives to work and increasing the attractiveness of low paid work. The Working Families' Tax Credit (WFTC) which was recently introduced in the UK is the most radical such experiment to be found in Europe. It is therefore of great relevance to the Irish case. This is especially so given that measures have already been taken here to move to a system of tax credits. In the remainder of this chapter we treat the WFTC along the lines of a case study, engaging in a discussion of its merits in the Irish context.

The utility of the WFTC, like any other policy measure, lies not only in its capacity to deliver on one policy objective but rather to deliver on a number. The following are in our view the critical aspects determining the measure's utility and relevance for Ireland: labour supply effects; work incentives; workless households; gender equity; poverty and low income; joint v. individual assessment. Consideration of them raises a host of general as well as specific issues.

6.2.4.1 Labour Supply

Ireland has recently been experiencing significant labour supply constraints. Hence a WFTC-type approach is relevant and attractive to Ireland for its general potential to increase labour supply. However, in a climate where concerns about emerging labour shortages vie for attention with the more traditional goal of overcoming long-term unemployment, it is not just quantity that matters but also quality. In the latter regard, the utility of the WFTC as a targeted measure is contingent to a very real extent on the individuals/groups it is likely to attract into the labour force. The available evidence suggests that these are in the Irish case likely to be at the low end of the skills spectrum.[93] The enticement of low-skilled workers into the labour force would only partially solve Ireland's labour supply problems since skill shortages and job vacancies are spread across the skills spectrum.

6.2.4.2 Incentives to Work

Both social welfare and tax policy have been and are active in seeking to increase the incentive to work. For almost ten years now, public policy has sought to reduce marginal tax rates and especially in recent years to cut the amount of tax paid by those with low earnings. As we have seen, relatively generous changes have also been made to Ireland's in-work benefit – the Family Income Supplement – as well as to other social security programmes. The Employment Action Plans over the last years reiterate the government's commitment to increase the reward for work. The implementation of a full tax credit system in April 2001 is part of this policy.[94] Some research exists on the possible incentive effects of different approaches, although not on the tax credit system itself. The minimum wage, for example, introduced in April, 2000, has been estimated to lead to an increase in the female participation rate of 3 per cent (compared to 1.5 for men) (Callan and Doris, 1999). It is mainly people with low education, especially those who have no education beyond primary school, who are expected to be attracted into the labour market by the minimum wage. The general thrust of the research on work incentives is that married women have the highest responsiveness to financial incentives. However, all predictions have to be put in the context of the huge rise which has taken place in married women's employment participation rate, from around 17 per cent in 1980 to around 45 per cent today. Hence it is not surprising that the wage elasticity for married women is believed to have fallen significantly between the mid-1980s and the mid-1990s (Callan and Dorris, 1999). There is, then, less scope for future expansion of the female labour force than there once was.

Within-couple decision making and employment-related behaviour are critical to the likely labour market effects of a WFTC approach. Little or nothing is known about intra-couple dynamics in Ireland other than some work by Callan et al (1998) which gives an indication of the identity of the women who are in employment. This work indicates that it is women married to low-earning men who have most increased their labour force participation in the last years. This again gives pause for reflection on the likely effectiveness of a WFTC in raising Irish labour supply in itself and in the desired direction. Given that lone parents have been the primary beneficiaries in the UK, any analysis of the Irish case must also take the situation of this target group into account. The employment participation rate of lone mothers with children under 15 years in Ireland was 52 per cent in 1997.[95] This, comparing favourably with the rate of their married counterparts at 48.8 per cent, sets Ireland in line with European patterns but places it ahead of the UK (at 44 per cent). There does not appear to be a problem of 'worklessness' among lone-parent beneficiaries of social payments (Department of Social, Community and Family Affairs, 2000). However a high level of part-time and/or low-paid work is indicated.[96] While we cannot be sure, it is unlikely that the social security provisions in Ireland are acting to trap lone-parent recipients in part-time, low-paid employment since earnings are not concentrated just below threshold levels (Department of Social, Community and Family Affairs, p. 79), though the earnings capacity of the mother may be at issue. As Bryson, Ford and White (1997, p. 8) say in relation to Britain: 'women with low qualifications have relatively low earnings capacity while those bringing up young children are performing an economically valuable and socially vital function'. It is also indicated that the decisions of Irish lone parents about employment are influenced as much by the amount of their combined welfare/work income as they are by the stability and security of that income (McCashin, 1996). In other words, the risks involved to a stable, if low, income are critical and these are evaluated not just in material terms but also in terms of the risks and 'losses' to family life.

The overall picture, then, with regard to the WFTC's impact on lone parents' employment is that: (a) the measure may be less effective in Ireland than it has been in the UK in increasing the participation rates of lone parents given their already high levels of activity, and (b) the goal of increasing lone parents' employment rate may be less important in Ireland.

6.2.4.3 Workless Households

Some 15 per cent of households with children in Ireland have no attachment to the labour market (Micklewright and Stewart, 2000, p. 26). The proportion in the UK is considerably higher at almost one in five. Developments in the Irish labour market in recent years have been dominated by extremely rapid growth in employment. Between 1994 and 1998 total employment rose by over 22 per cent, one of the highest growth rates in the industrialised world. Unemployment is at an all-time low (down to around 4 per cent) and a concerted set of active labour market programmes together with expanding employment opportunities have eaten away at the numbers in receipt of unemployment payments. As indicated above, even the majority (61 per cent) of recipients of lone-parent benefits are economically active. Hence one of the originating impulses for the introduction of the WFTC in the UK is not a problem in the Irish context at the present time (although it was of greater concern in the past).

6.2.4.4 Gender Equality

Gender equality is crucial to Ireland, in its own right and also as a partial solution to the labour supply problems. With the recent and very rapid increases in female participation, Ireland is no longer a European laggard (with a female participation rate of 46 per cent compared to the average EU rate of 46.5 per cent). However the participation rate of women aged between 25 and 54 years at 63 per cent is still considerably below the EU-15 average (71.6 per cent). Hence a WFTC-type approach may be advantageous to Ireland were it to succeed in encouraging more women into the labour force since this may help with moves towards gender equity as well as to ease the labour supply problem. However it is difficult to interpret the gender effects (as regards labour supply anyway) of the WFTC. In fact, two of the main studies completed (Gregg et al, 1999; Blundell et al, 2000) give diverging estimates of the WFTC's effects on women's and men's employment. While all the research predicts an unambiguous growth in the employment rate of lone parents, Gregg et al predict that the WFTC will primarily affect men's employment whereas the Blundell et al results suggest that the effects will be overwhelmingly on female employment. From the Irish perspective, the gender effects are important. Ireland has recently introduced gender mainstreaming which means that all new policies have to be gender proofed. In any event, the prediction by Blundell et al (2000) that significant numbers of men and women will exit the labour market once their partner enters is very important and needs to be carefully considered. This level of exit suggests a need to be conscious, when designing policy, of the disincentive effects for the second partner. The implications pertain not just to the distribution of employment between women and men but also to individual and household levels of wellbeing and income.

The matter of part-time employment is also relevant in this context. With some 17 per cent of all workers working on a part-time basis, the Irish economy has considerably less part-time employment compared with the UK. Given this, it is unsurprising that fewer employed Irish women work on a part-time basis compared with their UK counterparts, 30 per cent and 45 per cent respectively. However there is a trend towards part-time employment among Irish women – 58 per cent of the increase in women's employment between 1992 and 1998 was in part-time work. While the association of employment growth with part-time jobs is something of an international trend, it is not clear that growth of part-time employment is fully in accord with Irish national employment objectives. Hence, if a WFTC were to act to increase part-time and low-paid work, it may prove unattractive to Irish policy makers who have generally sought to realise a high skill/high wage vision for the economy. An equally undesirable outcome would be the ghettoisation of women in low-paid, part-time jobs. In this regard the levels of the tax credit are undoubtedly critical.

6.2.4.5 Poverty and Income Inequality

This is a very important issue for Ireland where massive economic growth has co-existed with very high poverty rates and significant income inequality. The latest figures suggest that some 25 per cent of all households were in 1998 below a poverty line set at 50 per cent of average income (Layte et al, 2000). Depending on the equivalence scale used, this represents an increase of between 10 and 22 per cent on the previous year. Given this and stated government commitment to overcoming such poverty levels, a WFTC-type approach would be very attractive in Ireland from an anti-poverty or anti-income inequality perspective. Results reported by Dilnot and McCrae (1999) suggest that the WFTC is a very well targeted form of redistribution, being especially good at directing extra money to low paid families with children. While there is some evidence of a shift in the composition of poor Irish households away from those with children towards childless households, child and family poverty continues to be a major policy issue in Ireland.

6.2.4.6 Joint versus Individual Assessment

With the changes announced in the budgets in the last two years, the government has committed itself to individualisation of the tax system. The WFTC, as a joint system, is therefore contrary to the planned development trajectory. This is something which is pertinent to social security as well. Up to now the Irish social security system has generally been oriented to households rather than individuals but, as we have seen, some momentum is underway to reconsider this. There are other unit-related issues as well. The WFTC in the UK is oriented to the household but some kind of objectives need to be set out for individuals as well. This would be especially important from a gender equality perspective for example.

This discussion suggests that the utility of a tax credit approach is limited in Ireland in the present climate. However, its capacity to target low-income households is impressive.

Chapter 7

Overview and Conclusions

Social policy in Ireland has been very active on the family front over the last decade. An increasing concern with family is reflected in the setting up of the Commission on the Family, the creation of the Family Services Agency as a specialist agency on and for the family and the designation of a ministry of state with responsibility for children (attached to the Department of Health and Children). Children along with the elderly are two groups prioritised by the current government. One can see this reflected in recent policy – in the very large increases in child benefit over the last four years for example, in the resources made available for childcare services, in the continuing expansion of benefits for the care of the elderly and in the National Children's Strategy. One of the main themes of this report has been that these and other measures for individual sectors of the population must be examined, and provided for, within a larger set of contours relating to, in the first instance, families and in the second their role and place in society.

When we look back from the vantage point of 2002, we can see that there were three different stages of family policy in Europe in the twentieth century. The first family policies date from the late nineteenth and early twentieth centuries in France and Sweden (Kamerman and Kahn, 1994, p. 8). These reflected concern with economic and demographic developments affecting families (especially problems of low birth rates and low wages). But the first major stage in the development of family policies (institutionalisation and growth in family allowances) did not take place until after World War II. The next major phase of expansion was in the 1960s, associated with the rediscovery of poverty. This gave the rationale for a general expansion of social protection systems and concerted efforts were made to support families (including those with only one parent). One could identify the 1990s as the third phase of European family policy. While most societies appear to have been conscious that their approach to the family might be outdated, it is only in the last two decades or so that European countries have got around to changing their policy profile. These changes have had five main foci.

One is care. Now, European countries are finding that they have to target the general exigencies of providing care for children and for the elderly rather than, as in the past, particular types of families. It matters less and less whether parents are married to each other or whether they live with the child, for example. It is, rather, more important that they meet their caring responsibilities and that the state is seen to help and encourage them in that. Social policy is assuming a greater role in mediating the relationship between paid and unpaid work; the relationship between cash and care is becoming central. No longer can European states assume that the caring will be automatically provided by the family. Associated with this is a move away from a focus on the family as an institution or unit to family relations and activities as existing outside, and increasingly outliving, the formal structure of marriage.

The second focus of recent family policy is what might be called 'children's liberation.' Children have moved if not to centre stage then certainly to the foreground of family policy in Europe. There is an observable trend towards a children's policy in which the wellbeing and welfare of children is considered in its own right (rather than within the context of family and parental rights or obligations). Ireland is well-placed as regards this trend, especially in view of the National Children's Strategy. The Strategy places discussions about the place of children in Irish society in the context of citizenship. This is welcome, for in international comparison

Ireland has traditionally been a low provider for children. The development of the National Children's Strategy and other measures which increase the support for families with children are therefore exciting not just in their own terms but because they may lead the way to a discussion about the meaning of citizenship for adults in Ireland.

The third change is dual-earner families. A few years ago the issues involved here would have been framed in terms of women's liberation and gender equity. Now, within a context of increasing pressures on one-earner families, and women's wish to be both workers and mothers, public policies are required to facilitate what is called the 'reconciliation of work and family life.' As outlined in the last chapter, this has different policy interpretations. But what is inescapable about it is that it involves both a re-orientation of the meaning of family life for men and women and a new balance between the family, the state and the market with regard to the provision of care and arrangements for the use of time and the procurement of income. Prosperity in the new millenium is understood not just as financial wellbeing, but also as a way of living in which choice is uppermost. Choice in relation to preferred family form is an integral part of the contemporary understanding of choice. This gives social policy a new complexion, not least in that it challenges it to create the conditions whereby people will choose, in the first instance, to have children and, in the second, to live their lives in a manner which is consistent with a social definition of family. Families can no longer be regarded as private. This together with other developments has broadened the ambit of social policy and made family policy one of the most vibrant (and contested) areas of social policy in Europe. In a sense what could formerly be referred to as 'the black-box of the family' is being opened up.

A fourth objective underlying contemporary policy reform is to enhance the functioning of the family and the wellbeing of its individual members. Amidst worries about a decline in public standards, the quality of family relationships is a special concern of policy. In this kind of climate, policy attention is turning to how the family can be helped to function better. The role of parents, the skills required for parenting and the quality of the relationship between parents and their children are in the forefront. The New Labour government in the UK for example is of the view that parents need better training and support, especially to develop their sense of responsibility. It has instituted a broad-ranging series of measures towards these ends.[97] While the emphasis is somewhat different in Ireland, there has been a growth in service provision to support families (e.g., education, counselling and support-related services) oriented to enhancing the coping skills of individual family members and, through that, the functioning of families. The wellbeing of children and the child's best interests is another strong impulse of policy rhetoric, if not reform, today. In many countries (e.g. Germany and Sweden) childcare is being more closely integrated into early education and there is also a trend underway to guarantee young children a place in childcare or pre-school education regardless of their parents' circumstances (Germany, UK and Sweden).

A fifth motor of change is the need to revisit equity. Redistribution and greater social equality are long-standing objectives of the European social model. But, changing patterns of social life, in the context of social policy models which are slower to change than the societies they seek to service, mean that equity needs to be reconfigured. The risks which underpinned the classic social insurance model were largely defined in terms of men's labour market participation. While these risks are still important, those associated with family and 'private' life are now equally important. So, policies are challenged to make social provision for a society in which women and children can no longer rely on a long-term basis on men to provide for them. As well as gender equity there is the thorny matter of the general balance that should exist between horizontal and vertical equity as objectives of social policy.

Against this background of change, it is interesting to consider the role of the EU. The EU was, according to Gauthier (1996, pp.148-9), one of two main international actors[98] to have contributed to the increasing visibility of the family as a political issue since the mid-1970s. Indeed, the European Parliament helped to circulate the term 'family policy' by adopting a resolution in 1983 which stressed the need to take into account the aspects of Community policy which affected the family and encouraging member states to adopt policies which took account of the multiple needs of families. As well as setting set up the Observatory on National Family Policies in 1989, with the task of monitoring the development of family policy in each of the member states and producing an annual report, another action taken by the European Commission was to issue a communication in 1989. This identified five sectors which would require regular concerted action at Community level, including lone parent families, deprived families, the reconciliation of work and family life, evaluation of the impact of family policies on the family and the inclusion and consideration of the family dimension in the establishment of appropriate Community policies. Of these, the EU is most associated with a commitment to reconciling work and family life. In one of its most recent initiatives in social policy – the social inclusion process which was decided on in 2000 and put into effect in 2001 – 'preserving family solidarity' is mentioned as one way of preventing the risk of social exclusion.[99] The meaning of 'family solidarity' has not been developed further to date.

Each country has its own pattern and unique history of social policy. Ireland's, as we have seen, was in the past marked by a relatively low provision of financial and other forms of support for families with children, as well as a generally high degree of reliance on the family to take care of the needs of its individual members (whatever they might be). The Irish policy profile is changing quite radically though, not just in terms of content but also as regards its strategic orientation. The family is central to contemporary policy development in Ireland, and what the analysis of this area of policy shows above all is that matters of the family can rival other concerns, such as employment levels, in forging a new social policy model in Ireland.

Footnotes

1. The Constitution is important in any analysis of Irish social policy because it contains a series of directive principles of social policy. These provide the foundations for social citizenship in Ireland. These principles pertain to the right to legal equality, the family, education, private property and religion.

2. A core grouping of articles is relevant in this context. Article 41.1.1 reads: 'The State recognises the Family as the natural primary and fundamental unit group of Society and as a moral institution possessing inalienable and imprescriptible rights, antecedent and superior to all positive law'.
   Article 41.1.2 reads: 'The State, therefore, guarantees to protect the Family in its constitution and authority, as the necessary basis of social order and as indispensable to the welfare of the Nation and the State'.
   Article 41.3.1 reads: 'The State pledges itself to guard with special care the institution of Marriage, on which the Family is founded, and to protect it against attack'.

3. These were very significant forerunners of the family allowances which would be introduced two decades later. As Montanari (2000, p. 310) points out with regard to European countries in general, in introducing child benefits for civil servants the state acting as an employer was taking the lead in implementing a family wage.

4. However the father could if he wished nominate the mother or another adult to obtain payment. According to Farley (1964, p. 72) this power to nominate was very frequently used.

5. Up until 1973, women were usually expected to give up employment upon marriage.

6. In addition to the personal allowance for single persons.

7. From the early 1920s up to 1980, the tax allowance for married couples was less than twice the allowance for a single person, except for the years 1951-52 and 1955-56 when the allowance for married couples was exactly twice that of a single person.

8. Although at that stage it was usually claimed on the father's insurance rather than on that of the mother.

9. It was confined to women working at least eighteen hours a week and excluded women on contracts of fewer than twenty-six weeks.

10. Paradigm as used by Fahey refers to both the explicit ideas about policy (such as formal statements of principles or objectives) as well as unspoken assumptions and values which shape the way issues are viewed, the types of language which are available to talk about these issues and the implicit identification of the groups, sources of information and types of discourse which are authoritative in defining problems and proposing solutions (1998, p. 385).

11. Support for such a general position is also to be found in the Irish Constitution. The Directive Principle of Social Policy (Art. 45.2) states that: 'The State shall in particular direct its social policy towards securing: that the citizens (all of whom, men and women equally, have the right to an adequate means of livelihood) may through their occupations find the means of making reasonable provision for their domestic needs.'

12. It was also increased if the family was headed by a single father but not to the same extent.

13. Wennemo (1994, p. 9) is of the view that family support to public employees, which was introduced in Ireland in 1926, should be viewed as part of the wage system and not primarily as a family benefit.

14. This continuum is bounded at each end by two extreme forms: the authoritarian and *laissez faire*. The former is equivalent to social engineering in which the state is extremely *dirigiste* while in the latter the state has no position or interest in the family. Given that these are so removed from existing practices in any society they are excluded from the discussion here.

15. It should also be pointed out that, given that the childcare sector has developed in Ireland in a very ad hoc manner and has not been closely regulated by the public authorities, the National Childcare Strategy was concerned about prevailing employment and other conditions. It therefore proposed a whole series of recommendations to regularise, regulate and upgrade the operation of the sector as a domain of employment and service provision.

16. Responsibility for childcare is quite fragmented in Ireland, being dispersed among a number of agencies. In order to deal with this problem, an important step towards a more co-ordinated approach was taken with the establishment in 1999 of a new administrative organisation of childcare, led by the Department of Justice, Equality and Law Reform, and designed to co-ordinate the delivery of childcare services over the course of the National Development Plan (2000-2006).

17. Extended care facilities include: (a) health board geriatric homes/hospitals, welfare homes, and long-stay beds in district/community hospitals, (b) voluntary homes and hospitals, and (c) private nursing homes.

18. Over the period 1990-1997, €82.5 million was spent on implementing the Act.

19. Until 1998, the family mediation and marriage and child counselling services were the responsibility of the Department of Justice, Equality and Law Reform.

20. A number of EU member states (or units thereof) have already established a Children Ombudsman/Office for Children's Rights including Austria, Belgium, Denmark, Finland, France, Portugal, Spain, Sweden and Wales. Countries outside the EU with a similar type of provision include Hungary, Iceland, Lithuania, Macedonia, Norway, Poland, Romania and Russia.

21. The average duration of claiming is estimated at 7.5 years (Department of Social, Community and Family Affairs, 2000, p. 23).

22. Asylum seekers have been excluded from entitlement since 1996.

23. The higher rate of child benefit for lone parents was abolished in 1998 for new claimants. At present therefore, the higher rates apply only to old claimants.

24. These increases were financed by freezing tax allowances for married couples and lone parents.

25. The concept of family is the dominating reference in French policy (rather than, say, the well-being of the child). For that reason these cash payments will be denoted throughout as family allowances, for this is how they are known in France.

26. The deficit in family expenditure amounted to €1.5 billion in 1994 and €2 billion in 1995. Expenditure in the family sector represents around 3.5 per cent of GDP. It is the only sector of social protection to have seen a percentage decrease in spending since 1959 (INSEE, 1996).

27. It is estimated that 310,000 families were affected by the measure, losing an average of €1,981.8 of their annual disposable income. However, since most of these families belonged to the highest-income decile, the loss represented only 2.4 per cent of their total income (Thelot and Villac, 1998).

28. Twenty-one if unemployed or 27 if in full-time education.

29. In other words, since the reform came into effect, the value of the child benefit is not tied to income.

30. The amount of the benefit, calculated by the employer, is subtracted from the income tax and in the case of a positive residual amount is paid out directly with wages.

31. This allowed, as of June 2001, childcare expenses of up to £135 (€219) a week for one child and £200 (€325.3) a week for two children to be written off against tax liability.

32. Formerly, Family Credit recipients who were also receiving child maintenance were only entitled to a disregard of £15 (€24.4) a week.

33. Only one credit exists for each family, payable to the partner with the highest income. If the partner who receives the credit does not pay sufficient tax to use all the credit, he or she will be able to transfer the unused credit to the other partner after the end of the tax year.

34. The *Quotient Familial* operates by attributing fiscal units or semi-units to each member of a family according to its composition. Each family is then taxed according to its total income divided by the total number of units, to which the corresponding tax rate is individually applied. In the allocation of units, each member of the couple is given one unit (*Quotient Conjugal*) and a half a unit is given for each child. Large families are given additional allowances – a full unit is allotted for the third and each subsequent child. Lone parents are also treated specially – one unit is allotted for all children except the second (for whom half a unit is allowed).

35. The CNAF (*Caisse Nationale des Allocations Familiales*) is an independent branch of social security responsible for the financial administration and management of the family benefits.

36. So, for example, a family with three children with an annual income of €15,244 does not benefit from the system (since it is not liable to tax) while the allowance for a family of similar composition but with an annual income of €106,714 amounts to €8,903.

37. With the reform, maintenance is treated in a way that makes employment more attractive. At present, for recipients of either Income Support or Job Seeker's Allowance all maintenance received counts as income and so is deducted against the benefit, whereas recipients of in-work benefits have been entitled to a maintenance disregard of £15 (€24.4) a week since 1993.

38. Yet, on the other hand, economic activity rates among lone mothers are significantly higher than those of women living in couples with the same number of children and, when placed in a European perspective, they exceed those of most other EU country members.

39. The UK refused to sign the former on the grounds that it might price part-time workers out of the market and it opted out of the Parental Leave Directive on the grounds that this should be an area for negotiation between employers and employees.

40. The implementation of the Directive for pregnant workers brought changes in maternity benefits. In particular, the rates of both the Statutory Maternity Pay and the Maternity Allowance were increased, a 52-week qualifying period for Maternity Allowance was extended to 66 weeks and state reimbursement to employers was reduced to 92 per cent.

41. The government has set up a fund (Challenge Fund) to help employers to develop and implement reconciliation policies but this only covers the costs of consultancy advice.

42. By 'dependant' is meant parent, wife, husband, partner, child, or someone who lives as part of the family for whom the employee is the main carer.

43. Formerly, eligibility was based on the number of National Insurance contributions paid, so that women earning less than the lower earnings limit were not entitled to Maternity Allowance. With the new changes, the benefit is open to women earning between £30 (€48.8) and £67 (€109) and the payment is equivalent to 90 per cent of their average earnings.

44. Parents who do not qualify for the highest rate of parental leave benefit (that is, do not fulfil the condition of having been employed for at least 240 consecutive days before confinement) are entitled to a minimum guaranteed payment of 60 SEK (€6.6) a day. The sole condition of entitlement to this minimum amount is to have been insured for at least 180 consecutive days prior to the claim.

45. However, lower take-up rates also need to be set in the context of falling fertility rates during the decade.

46. In Sweden, both parents cannot be on parental leave at the same time.

47. When it was first introduced in 1985, eligibility was limited to parents who had been employed for at least two years within the two and a half years prior to the birth of the child. However, in 1987, the links with previous employment were loosened by making the benefit open to parents who had been employed for at least two years within any of the ten years prior to the birth of the child.

48. The full current amount of the payment (at a fixed rate of €485 per month) is equivalent to about 30 per cent of average individual monthly income.

49. In 1995, 42 per cent of part-time employees were on 'imposed' part-time contracts, most of them coming from low-income families and lone-parent families (Galtier, 1999). The sectors where this type of work has increased most rapidly are the retail and catering sectors, where women are the overwhelming majority of workers and the conditions are precarious (low pay and atypical working hours).

50. Private childcare in the home (the most flexible type of childcare) is very expensive – despite the existence of AGED, a benefit covering part of the social security costs of employment.

51. Since 1986 entitlement to the allowance was dependent on annual income after the seventh month (€15,032 for couples and €12,117 for lone parents). The new income limits for the first six months introduced in 1994 were €51,129 for couples and €38,346 for lone parents.

52. The past decade saw a significant decrease in the proportion of families receiving the parental allowance. For example, in 1987, 85 per cent of eligible families received the benefit compared with about 50 per cent in 1999. Only 1.5 per cent of all fathers eligible for parental leave actually took it in contrast to 90 per cent of all eligible mothers

53. This applies only to people working in firms with more than 15 employees.

54. The rationale for this lack of state involvement in childcare is that mothers have a choice about working outside the home and if they do so are responsible for making their own private arrangements.

55. More specifically, free early education for 3 and 4 year olds can be provided by primary schools, nursery schools, playgroups, day nurseries and a group of registered childminders.

56. In the UK as in Ireland, a strong distinction has traditionally been made between 'care' and 'education' of children, with different providers, aims and departmental responsibilities. The UK has in recent years, however, seen a general trend towards more integration.

57. A maximum fee of 700 SEK (€77.6) for the first child (aged 1 to 5) attending preschool and family care, and a maximum fee of 500 SEK (€55.4) for 6 to 12-year-olds enrolled in leisure centres or family daycare.

58. One problem with fees which vary with income is that some parents (mainly women, low income earners, parents with small children and lone mothers) may feel discouraged to convert part-time work into full-time work or the unemployed may be discouraged to take up employment. Given this, it has been argued that the long-term goal of the measures is to improve the Swedish economy (Jonsson, 2000).

59. In 1999, 35 per cent of families with at least one child under 11 years (and regularly receiving some sort of childcare service) used a paid service, in contrast to 22 per cent in 1984 and 31 per cent in 1995.

60. The right came into effect in January 1996 but with an interim implementation period until January 1999.

61. However they cannot be used to pay a spouse, partner or close relative living in the same household.

62. The pension age for women is 60 years, while for men it is 65 years.

63. These grants amounted to 3 SEK billion (€332 million) and were provided for a five-year period.

64. This benefit is reserved for bed-ridden people or those needing help several times a day to carry out essential daily activities. Excluded from this scheme are elderly people who, although they have maintained some degree of independence, still require assistance in performing daily tasks such as dressing, personal hygiene, cooking and so forth.

65. In 1992, 90 per cent of all care in the home was provided by family members.

66. In 1991, 40 per cent of the €15.3 billion spent on social assistance was used for long-term care.

67. The scheme is financed through contributions from both employers and employees. Employees' contributions are between 1.5 per cent and 2 per cent of gross earnings. Employers are compensated by a reduction in paid annual holidays of one day.

68. The international body established by the Convention to monitor its implementation on a worldwide basis.

69. In Northern Ireland there has been wide consultation with children and young people on the need for a Children's Commissioner.

70. Apart from the London's Children's Rights Commissioner which is a three-year project designed to demonstrate why it is essential that children in England have an independent children's rights commissioner.

71. The proposed Bill is selected from a set of ten, all of which have been drafted by children themselves (with the help of their teachers).

72. For example, in the year 2000, new legislation on the improvement and protection of river waters was passed through the children's parliament.

73. It is important to point out, though, that these guarantees should be regarded as statements of principle depending on available resources. Only in Finland can parents take the municipality to court if day care is not provided (Rostgaard and Fridberg, 1998, p. 39).

74. The income of spouses is added together and subject to different tax bands and rates to those applying to single individuals, while personal allowances are doubled.

75. This type of joint taxation adds the total income of spouses and divides it by a quotient which depends on family size. The resulting calculated tax for the family unit is then multiplied by the same quotient to arrive at a tax liability for adult family members. For families without children, the quotient method is equivalent to split taxation.

76. Spouses divide the total household income between them and it is taxed at a half rate for each.

77. Until 1996, families were entitled to both an income-related child benefit (*Kindergeld*) and a tax allowance per child. Since 1996, families must choose between them, depending on which provides the higher benefit. This change did not represent a reduction in the total benefit received by families, as it was accompanied by sharp increases in both the amounts of the child tax allowance and the *Kindergeld*.

78. The arrangements described in the study relate to the situation in each country as of May 1996.

79. Net income is defined as gross earnings less income tax and social security contributions payable on those earnings, plus cash benefits payable to the family (child benefit package). In calculating net income, health, school and housing costs were taken into account.

80. It is important to note that the value of the child benefit package does not include tax relief provision for married couples.

81. The following are the five model families utilised: couples and lone parents with one earner receiving half national average male earnings; couples and lone parents with one earner receiving national average male earnings; couples and lone parents with one earner receiving one and a half times national average male earnings; couples with one earner receiving national average male earnings and the other receiving 0.66 average female earnings; couples with one earner receiving one and a half times national average male earnings and the other receiving one and a half times average female earnings.

82. This is calculated after health and school costs and before housing costs. Note, however, that accounting for these costs did not alter the ranking.

83. Nolan (2000) tends to confirm these findings.

84. The total birth or fertility rate is an indicator of the expected average number of children per woman. Such data cannot be used to assess the impact of measures on the timing and spacing of births. For the latter types of analysis, information is needed on individual family and fertility histories. This kind of information is becoming more widely available but analyses of this type are most advanced in Sweden (Ronsen, 1999).

85. In France, people in receipt of the parental allowance are removed from the Live Register and classified as 'inactive' during the period of receipt.

86. However since the homecare allowance system was introduced in 1985, Finnish parents have had the possibility of taking extended leave with a limited payment.

87. The Programme for Prosperity and Fairness contains a commitment 'to produce proposals to progress the implementation of administrative individualisation within the social welfare system' (2000, p. 81).

88. In this regard, however, it is important to note that the level of 'worklessness' is not high among beneficiaries of the One-Parent Family Payment: 61 per cent of the 85,000 or so beneficiaries had earnings in the 1998/9 tax year (Department of Social, Community and Family Affairs, 2000). There is evidence of some dynamism also in that this represents an increase of 4 per cent on the previous year. However work is not the major source of income for these beneficiaries: 72 per cent of those with earnings had less than €7,618 (just around the threshold for earnings disregards). This can be taken to indicate a high level of part-time and/or low paid work.

89. The Review Group outlined several points to be considered in any future development in this direction. These are: (a) treatment of other 'stay at home' adults within the social welfare code, and (b) the needs of different categories of lone parents having different levels of education and work experience.

90. For example, the Review Group proposed the following measures: (a) interviews with job facilitators/FÁS personnel for recipients who are ready for employment and training opportunities, (b) access to education and training through FÁS, Back to Education and the Vocational Training Opportunities Scheme, (c) support with childcare, (d) grant aid to innovative programmes helping lone parents, and (e) an information campaign.

91. On the assumption that one member of the couple is receiving the One-Parent Family Payment and the other member is employed on low wages.

92. For a discussion of this in the Irish context see Ferguson, McKeown and Rooney (1998).

93. This is true especially of current beneficiaries of lone parent and unemployment benefits. It is known, for instance, that the general profile of the recipients of the One-Parent Family Payment are poorly educated, rather young, tend to have one child (although nearly 40 per cent have more than one child) and to be never married (Department of Social, Community and Family Affairs, 2000). The skill levels of the other populations targeted by WFTC – men and women living in households where the other partner is in or out of the labour market – is impossible to predict but is probably likely to be in the low to medium skills range.

94. A special working group to examine the role of refundable tax credits has also been set up as part of the latest national agreement between the government and the social partners (the Programme for Prosperity and Fairness).

95. This figure, the latest available, is likely to be higher at the present time given: (a) the continued expansion of the Irish labour market, and (b) the fact that the participation rate of lone mothers is known to have grown by 19 per cent in the two years between 1995 and 1997.

96. The finding of Bryson, Ford and White (1997, p. 43) to the effect that Family Credit in Britain acted as an incentive for lone mothers to take jobs at wage rates below what they are capable of getting is also important. Hence the advantage of helping more mothers to work is partly offset by the lower productivity of those receiving the benefit, including some who would have worked even without it. For them this kind of finding underlines the value of policies which would foster continuing education and training among lone parents.

97. Such as, for example, a parenting institute and a helpline for parents.

98. The other was the United Nations.

99. As part of this new initiative, each member state must compile and present its strategy for combating poverty and social exclusion in the form of a two-year national plan of action. Known as NAPs/incl (national action plans against poverty and social exclusion), the first round of this process (when states submitted plans for the July 2001 - June 2003 period), and received feedback on them in what is known as an open method of co-ordination, is already completed. The next round of national action plans is planned for 2003.

Appendix

Research Framework and Key Research Questions

The empirical part of the research project was organised around three stages. The first focused on identifying the nature of each country's family-related policy package. This part of the research addressed itself in the first instance to a general set of questions about each country's approach to the family and then to some of the historical details of provision. The second step was to identify how policies had changed in the last decade. The third stage of the research was to identify some of the impacts associated with policy. Existing research was mainly relied on here although we also carried out some direct comparisons of our countries on a range of indicators.

1. Characterising a Country's Family-related Policy Package

Background/Objectives of Policy

What are the pillars of policy towards the family in terms of
* aims and objectives of policy
* programmes
* policy instruments (cash benefits, services, tax allowances)?
What is the tradition of family policy in the country?

Institutional and other Parameters of Policy

How is policy on the family institutionalised (e.g. through a ministry of its own or as part of a ministry, what is the constitutional position as regards the family)?

Does a country have what could be called a family policy (in the sense of a designated, deliberate policy) or one on/which affects the family?

How wide does a concern with family extend across policy fields (in terms of the number and nature of policy arenas such as health, taxation, education, labour market)?

Who are/have been the main actors in relation to the family?

Details of Policy

To what extent can the country be said to have a policy in regard to the following broad headings:

- care (for children and adults)
- the wellbeing of children
- gender equity
- horizontal redistribution
- lone-parent families
- poverty/financial risk associated with rearing children?

And what is that policy and which policy instruments are utilised?

To what extent does policy on the family relate to/is understandable in terms of:

- a concern with families with children
- a concern with older people and their families
- reconciling work and family life
- motherhood
- survivorship
- reducing poverty among children/families with children
- providing for young people (teenagers and young adults)?

2.   Identifying Changes/Development

What has changed in the country's policy package (instruments, programmes, general objectives) in the last decade?

What principles or motives have guided the reforms?

To what extent can one identify a movement of family policy on a trajectory and how is one to characterise this trajectory:

- from specific to general measures (perhaps from field to perspective)
- from more to less generous and vice versa
- from a concern with the family as a collectivity to a focus upon the rights, entitlements and behaviour of individual family members
- from an implicit to an explicit family policy (or vice versa)
- from unidimensional to diversified support for families
- from a transfer to a service model (and vice versa)?

Where does the country stand in terms of the usually identified three stages of family policy (family allowances; more widespread support of families; care-oriented policies)?

Has the tradition/orientation of policy towards the family changed?

What is the economic context of reform?

What is the political context of reform?

3. Identifying Possible Impacts of Changes in Family Policies

Are there any identifiable changes in the following that appear to be associated with changes in policy

- the labour market participation of spouses/partners and of young family members
- family size/fertility rates
- horizontal income inequalities
- poverty rates?

Bibliography

Afsa, C. (1996), 'L'activité féminine á l'epreuve de l'allocation parentale d'éducation', *Recherches et Prévisions*, vol 46, pp. 1-8.

Atkinson, A., Bourguignon, S. and Chiappori, R. (1987), *The French Tax Benefit System and a Comparison with the British System*, London: Discussion Paper TIDI/106.

Bahle, T. (1995), *Familienpolitik in Westeuropa*, Frankfurt: Campus.

Bahle, T. and Rothenbacher, F. (1996), 'Germany' in European Observatory on National Family Policies, *Developments in National Family Policies in 1995*, York: Social Policy Research Unit, University of York.

Barbier, J.C. (1990), 'Comparing Family Policies in Europe: Methodological Problems', *International Social Security Review*, vol 3, pp. 326-41.

Bieback, K.J. (1992), 'Family Benefits: The New Legal Structures of Subsidizing the Family', *Journal of European Social Policy*, vol 2, no 4, pp. 239-54.

Blundell, R., Duncan, A., McCrae, J. and Meghir, C. (2000), 'The Labour Market Impact of the Working Families' Tax Credit', *Fiscal Studies*, vol 21, no 1, pp. 75-104.

Bouget, D. (1998), 'The Juppé Plan and the Future of the French Social Welfare System', *Journal of European Social Policy*, vol 8, no 2, pp. 155-72.

Bradshaw, J., Ditch, J., Holmes, H. and Whiteford, P. (1993), *Support for Children: A Comparison of Arrangements in Fifteen Countries*, London: HMSO.

Brannen, J. (1999), 'Reconsidering Children and Childhood: Sociological Perspectives', in Silva, E.B. and Smart, C. (eds), *The New Family?*, London: Sage.

Brouwer, I. and Wierda, E. (1998), 'The Combination Model: Child Care and the Part-time Labour Supply of Men in the Dutch Welfare State' in Schippers, J.J., Siegers, J.J. and de Jong-Gierveld, J. (eds), *Child Care and Female Labour Supply in the Netherlands*, Amsterdam: Thesis.

Bryson, A., Ford, R. and White, M. (1997), *Making Work Pay Lone Mothers, Employment and Well-being*, York: Joseph Rowntree Foundation.

Bundesministerium für Familie und Senioren (1993), *Zwölf Wege der Familienpolitik in der europäischen Gemeinschaft*, Schriftenreihe Band 22.1, Stuttgart: Kohlhammer.

Callan, T., Nolan, B., O'Neill, D. and Sweetman, O. (1998), *Female Labour Supply and Income Inequality in Ireland*, Maynooth: National University of Ireland Maynooth, Economics Department Working Papers Series, no 79/06/98.

Callan T. and Doris A. (1999), 'Labour Supply Responses', in *The Impact of the Minimum Wage in Ireland*, Final Report of the Interdepartmental Group of Implementation of National Minimum Wage, Dublin: Stationery Office.

Cohen, B. (1999), 'Parental leave in Europe: Policy implications', in Moss, P. and Deven, F. (eds), *Parental Leave: Progress or Pitfall?*, Brussels: NIDI/CBGS.

Combat Poverty Agency (2000), *Public Subvention of Childcare: An Anti-poverty Perspective*, Dublin: Combat Poverty Agency.

Commission on Social Welfare (1986), *Report of the Commission on Social Welfare*, Dublin: Stationery Office.

Commission on the Family (1996), *Strengthening Families for Life: Interim Report of the Commission on the Family to the Minister for Social, Community and Family Affairs*, Dublin: Department of Social, Community and Family Affairs.

Commission on the Family (1998), *Strengthening Families for Life: Final Report of the Commission on the Family to the Minister for Social, Community and Family Affairs*, Dublin: Stationery Office.

Commission on the Status of Women (1972), *Report of the Commission on the Status of Women,* Dublin: Stationery Office.

Coustitution of Ireland (Bunreacht na hÉireann (1937), Dublin: Stationery Office.

Cousins, M. (1995), *The Irish Social Welfare System Law and Social Policy*, Dublin: The Round Hall Press.

CREDOC (1999), *Le Devenir des Sortants de líAllocation parentale d'Èducation de Rang 2,* Collection des Rapports No. 202. Paris: CREDOC/CNAF.

Curry, J. (1993), *Irish Social Services*, 2nd edition, Dublin: Institute of Public Administration.

Daly, M. (1998), 'A More Caring State? The Implications of Welfare State Restructuring for Social Care in the Republic of Ireland', in Lewis, J. (ed) *Gender, Social Care and Welfare State Restructuring in Europe,* Aldershot: Ashgate.

Daly, M. (1999), 'The Functioning Family: Catholicism and Social Policy in Germany and Ireland', *Comparative Social Research*, vol 18, pp. 105-33.

Daly, M. (2000), 'A Fine Balance? Women's Labour Market Participation Patterns in International Comparison', in Scharpf, F. and Schmidt, V. (eds), *From Vulnerability to Competitiveness: Welfare and Work in the Open Economy*, vol II, Oxford: Oxford University Press.

Daly, M. and Lewis, J. (1998), 'Introduction: Conceptualising Social Care in the Context of Welfare State Restructuring', in Lewis, J. (ed) *Gender, Social Care and Welfare State Restructuring in Europe*, Aldershot: Ashgate.

Department of Health and Children (2000) *Health Statistics 1999*, Dublin: Stationery Office.

Department of Social Welfare (1996) Report of Conferance Proceedings 'Beyond Equel Treatment, Social Security in a Changing Europe', held in Dublin Castle, 10-12 October, Dublin: Department of Social Welfare.

Department of Social, Community and Family Affairs (1998), *Review of Carer's Allowance*, Dublin: Department of Social, Community and Family Affairs.

Department of Social, Community and Family Affairs (2000), *Review of the One-Parent Family Payment*, Dublin: Stationery Office.

Department of Social, Community and Family Affairs (2001), *Statistical Information on Social Welfare Services 2000*, Dublin: Stationery Office.

Descolonges, M. and Fagnani, J. (1998), *La Flexibilité dans l'Emploi: Un Moyen de Concilier sa Vie professionelle et sa Vie familiale ou une nouvelle Forme de Précarité? (Le cas de la France)*, Brussels: European Commission DG V.

Dex, S. and Joshi, H. (1999), 'Careers and Motherhood: Policies for Compatibility', *Cambridge Journal of Economics*, vol 23, pp. 641-59.

Dilnot, A. and McCrae, J. (1999), *Family Credit and the Working Families' Tax Credit*, London: Institute for Fiscal Studies, Briefing Note No 3.

Euronet at http://europeanchildrensnetwork.gla.ac.uk.

European Commission (2000), *Social Protection in the Member States of the European Union: Situation on January 1st 2000 and Evolution* (MISSOC), Employment and Social Affairs Series, Luxembourg: Office for Official Publications of the European Communities.

European Commission Network on Childcare (1996), *A Review of Services for Young Children in the European Union 1990-1995*, Brussels: European Commission Directorate General V.

European Industrial Relations Observatory at http://www.eiro.ie.

European Observatory on National Family Policies (1998), *A Synthesis of National Family Policies in 1996*, Brussels: European Commission Employment and Social Affairs.

Eurostat (2000), *Eurostat Yearbook: A Statistical Eye on Europe*, Luxembourg: Office for Official Publications of the European Communities.

Expert Working Group on Childcare (1999), *National Childcare Strategy*, Dublin: Stationery Office.

Expert Working Group on the Integration of the Tax and Social Welfare Systems (1996), *Integrating Tax and Social Welfare*, Dublin: Stationery Office.

Fagnani, J. (1998), 'Helping Mothers to Combine Paid and Unpaid Work – or Fighting Unemployment? The Ambiguities of French Family Policy', *Community, Work and Family*, vol 1, no 3, pp. 297-312.

Fahey, T. (1997), *The Elderly, the Family and the State in Ireland, Report to the Joint Committee on the Family, Houses of Oireachtas*, Dublin: Stationery Office.

Fahey, T. (1998), 'Family Policy in Ireland – A Strategic Overview, Background Paper for the Commission on the Family' in Commission on the Family, *Strengthening Families for Life*, Dublin: Stationery Office.

Fahey, T. and Murray, P. (1994), *Health and Autonomy among the Over-65s in Ireland*, Dublin: National Council for the Elderly.

Fahey, T. and Fitz Gerald, J. (1997), *Welfare Implications of Demographic Trends*, Dublin: Oak Tree Press.

Fahey, T. and Russell, H. (2001), *Family Formation in Ireland: Trends, Data Needs and Implications*, Dublin: Economic and Social Research Institute, Policy Research Series, No 43.

Familles de France at http://www.famillesdefrance.asso.fr.

Farley, D. (1964), *Social Insurance and Social Assistance in Ireland*, Dublin: Institute of Public Administration.

Ferguson, H., McKeown, K. and Rooney, D. (1998), *Changing Fathers? Fatherhood and Family Life in Modern Ireland*, Cork: The Collins Press.

Foley, P., Roche, J. and Tucker, S. (eds) (2001), *Children in Society Contemporary Theory, Policy and Practice*, Basingstoke: Palgrave.

Fox Harding, L. (1996), *Family, State and Social Policy*, Basingstoke: Macmillan.

Galtier, B. (1999), 'Le Temps Partiels: Entre Emplois choisis et Emplois 'faute de mieux''', *Économie et Statistique*, 322, pp. 57-77.

Gauthier, A.H. (1996), *The State and the Family: A Comparative Analysis of Family Policies in Industrialized Countries*, Oxford: Clarendon Press.

Gauthier, A.H. (1999), 'Historical Trends in State Support for Families in Europe (post 1945)', *Children and Youth Services Review*, vol 21, no 11/12, pp. 937-65.

Gauthier, A.H. and Hatzius, J. (1997), 'Family Benefits and Fertility: An Econometric Analysis', *Population Studies*, vol 51, pp. 295-306.

Gillot, D. (1998), *Pour une Politique de la Famille Renové*, Paris: La Documentation Française.

Gornick, J.C., Meyers, M.K. and Ross, K.E. (1997), 'Supporting the Employment of Mothers: Policy Variation across Fourteen Welfare States', *Journal of European Social Policy*, vol 7, no 1, pp. 45-70.

Government of Sweden (1998), *Strategy for Giving Effect in Sweden to the UN Convention on the Rights of the Child*, Stockholm: Government of Sweden.

Gregg, P., Johnson, P. and Reed, H. (1999), *Entering Work and the British Tax and Benefit System*, London: IFS.

Gustafsson, S., Wetzels, C., Vlasbom, J. and Dex, S. (1996), 'Women's Labour Force Transitions in Connection with Childbirth: A Panel Data Comparison between Germany, Sweden and Great Britain', *Journal of Population Economics*, vol 9, no 3, pp. 223-46.

Hantrais, L. and Letablier, M. (1996), *Families and Family Policies in Europe*, Harlow: Longman.

INED (1999), 'Les Chômeurs dans leur Famille', *Population et Sociétés*, no. 350.

INSEE (1996), 'La Protection Sociale', *Insee Premiére*, no. 461.

Hoem, J. (1992), *Public Policy as the Fuel of Fertility: Effects of a Policy Reform on the Pace of Childbearing in Sweden in the 1980s*, Stockholm: Stockholm University, Stockholm Research Reports in Demography no 69.

Howard, M. (1999), 'Child Benefit - Where Next?' *Poverty*, 103, pp. 8-11.

Innocenti Research Centre (2000), *A League Table of Child Poverty in Rich Nations Innocenti Report Card,* No. 1, Florence: UNICEF Innocenti Research Centre.

International Social Security Review (1994), vol 47, nos 3-4.

Ireland Employment Action Plan 2000.

Ireland National Development Plan 2000-2006, Dublin: Stationery Office.

Jenson, J. and Sincau, M. (1995), Francios Mitteraud et les Françaises: Un Rendez-vous Marqué? Paris: Presses de de la Fondation Nationale des Sciences Politiques.

Jenson, J. and Sineau, M. (1998), 'Qui Doit Garder le jeune Enfant?', *Recherches et Prévisions*, vol 53, pp. 1-21.

Jonsson, I. (2000), 'Fixed Rates for Childcare in Sweden. A Reform Proposal' (unpublished manuscript).

Joshi, H. and Davies, H. (1992), 'Day Care in Europe and Mothers' Forgone Earnings', *International Labour Review*, vol 32, no 6, pp. 561-579.

Kamerman, S.B. and Kahn, A.J. (eds) (1978), *Family Policy: Government and Families in Fourteen Countries*, New York: Columbia University Press.

Kamerman, S.B. and Kahn, A.J. (1994), 'Family Policy and the under-3s: Money, Services, and Time in a policy package', *International Social Security Review*, vol 47, nos 3-4, pp. 31- 43.

Kaufmann, F.X. (1990), *Zukunft der Familie: Stabilität, Stabilitätsrisiken und Politischen Bedingungen*, Beck: M‚ nchen.

Jauson, J.and Sincau, M. (1995), Francois Mitterand et les Fransçaises: Un Rendez-vous Marquè? Paris: Presses de la Foudation Nationale des Sciences Politiques.

Kaufmann, F.X (1993), 'Familienpolitik in Europa' in Bundesministerium für Familie und Senioren, (eds), *40 Jahre Familienpolitik in der Bundesrepublik Deutschland: Rückblick - Ausblick*, Neuwied: Luchterhand.

Kautto, M., Heikkila, M., Hivinden, B., Marklund, S. and Ploug, N. (eds) (1999), *Nordic Social Policy: Changing Welfare States*, London: Routledge.

Kennedy, F. (1989), *Family, Economy and Government in Ireland*, Dublin: Economic and Social Research Institute Paper No. 143.

Lansdown, G. (2001), 'Children's Welfare and Children's Rights', in Foley, P., Roche, J. and Tucker, S. (eds), *Children in Society Contemporary Theory, Policy and Practice*, Basingstoke: Palgrave.

Layte, R., Maitre, B., Nolan, B., Watson, D., Williams, J. and Casey, B. (2000), *Monitoring Poverty Trends: Results from the 1998 Living in Ireland Survey*, Dublin: Economic and Social Research Institute Working Paper No 132.

Letablier, M.T. and Rieucau, G. (2000), 'The Policy Logics of Action about Caring for Children', paper presented at 4th Seminar of the TSER Network Working and Mothering: Social Practices and Social Policies, Paris, March 23-25.

Lewis, J. (1992), 'Gender and the Development of Welfare Regimes', *Journal of European Social Policy*, vol 2, no 3, pp. 159-73.

Lewis, S. (1999), 'Work-family Arrangements in the UK', in Den Dulk, L., Van Doorne-Huiskes, A. and Schippers, J. (eds), *Work-Family Arrangements in Europe*, Amsterdam: Thela Thesis.

Lüscher, K., Schultheis, F. and Wehrspaun, M. (eds) (1990), *Die 'postmoderne' Familie: Familiale Strategien und Familienpolitik in einer Übergangszeit*, Konstanz: Universitätsverlag Konstanz.

Maguire, M. (1986), 'Ireland' in Flora, P. (ed) *Growth to Limits The Western European Welfare States Since World War II*, vol 2, Berlin: de Gruyter.

Makrinioti, D. (1994), 'Conceptualization of Childhood in a Welfare State: A Critical Reappraisal', in Qvortrup, J., Bardy, M., Sgritta, G. and Wintersberger, H. (eds) *Childhood Matters Social Theory, Practice and Politics*, Aldershot: Avebury.

Martin, C., Math, A. and Renaudat, E. (1998), 'Caring for very Young Children and Dependent Elderly people in France: Towards a commodification of social care?', in Lewis, J. (ed.), *Gender, Social Care and Welfare State Restructuring in Europe*, Aldershot: Ashgate.

Martin, F. (2000), *The Politics of Children's Rights*, Cork: Cork University Press.

McCashin, A. (1996), *Lone Mothers in Ireland A Local Study*, Dublin: Oak Tree Press.

McCashin, A. (1999), 'The Policy Challenge in Reforming the Tax/Welfare Treatment of Households', paper prepared for the Combat Poverty Agency/Department of Social, Community and Family Affairs Policy Seminar on 'The Tax/Welfare Treatment of Households', 10 December, Dublin Castle.

McLaughlin, E. (1993), 'Ireland: Catholic Corporatism', in Cochrane, A. and Clarke, J. (eds), *Comparing Welfare States: Britain in International Context*, London: Sage.

McLaughlin, E. (1999), 'Economic Independence and Individualisation', paper prepared for the Combat Poverty Agency/Department of Social, Community and Family Affairs Policy Seminar on Tax/Welfare Treatment of Households, 10 December, Dublin Castle.

Meyer, T. (1994), *Kinder, Kirche, Kapitalismus. Warum es im deutschen Sozialstaat einen Kindergartennotstand gibt,* Berlin: WZB Discussion Paper FSI 94 - 210.

Micklewright, J. and Stewart, K. (2000), *The Welfare of Europe's Children: Are EU Member States Converging?,* Bristol: The Policy Press.

Montanari, I. (2000), 'From Family Wage to Marriage Subsidy and Child Benefits: Controversy and Consensus in the Development of Family Policy', *Journal of European Social Policy,* vol 10, no 4, pp. 307-33.

Moss, P. and Deven, F. (eds) (1999), *Parental Leave: Progress or Pitfall?,* Brussels: NIDI/CBGS.

Nasman, E. (1999), 'Work-family Arrangements in Sweden' in Den Dulk, L., Van Doorne-Huiskes, A. and Schippers, J. (eds), *Work-Family Arrangements in Europe,* Amsterdam: Thela Thesis.

National Children's Strategy, (2000), Dublin: Stationery Office.

National Economic and Social Council (1999), *Opportunities, Challenges and Capacities for Choice,* Dublin: NESC.

Nolan, B. (2000), *Child Poverty in Ireland,* Dublin: Oak Tree Press.

Olah, L. Sz. (1998), *Do Public Policies Influence Fertility? Evidence from Sweden and Hungary from a Gender Perspective,* Stockholm: Demographic Unit, Stockholm University, Stockholm Research Reports in Demography No 130.

Oldman, D. (1994), 'Adult-child Relations as Class Relations', in Qvortrup, J., Bardy, M., Sgritta, G. and Wintersberger, H. (eds), *Childhood Matters Social Theory, Practice and Politics,* Aldershot: Avebury.

O'Shea, E. Donnison, D. and Larragy, J. (1991), *The Role and Future Development of Nursing Homes in Ireland,* Dublin: National Council for the Elderly.

Ostner, I. (1997), 'Lone Mothers in Germany before and after Unification' in Lewis, J. (ed), *Lone Mothers in European*

Welfare Regimes: Shifting Policy Logics, London: Jessica Kingsley.

Ostner, I. (1998), 'The Politics of Care Policies in Germany', in Lewis, J. (ed), *Gender, Social Care and Welfare State Restructuring in Europe*, Aldershot: Ashgate.

Plumb, M. and Walsh, J. (2000), 'Child Income Support: Options for Policy Reform', in Barrett, A. (ed), *Budget Perspectives Proceedings of a Conference held on 19 September 2000*, Dublin: Economic and Social Research Institute.

Powell, F.W. (1992), *The Politics of Irish Social Policy*, Lewiston/Queenston/Lampeter: Edwin Mellen.

Programme for Prosperity and Fairness (2000), Dublin: Stationery Office.

Qvortrup, J. (1994), 'Childhood Matters: An Introduction' in Qvortrup, J., Bardy, M., Sgritta, G. and Wintersberger, H. (eds), *Childhood Matters Social Theory, Practice and Politics*, Aldershot: Avebury.

Report of the Working Group Examining the Treatment of Married, Cohabiting and One-Parent Families under the Tax and Social Welfare Codes, (1999), Dublin: Stationery Office.

Ronsen, M. (1998), *Fertility and Public Policies – Evidence from Norway and Finland*, Oslo: Statistics Norway, Document 98/12.

Ronsen, M. (1999), 'Assessing the Impacts of Parental Leave: Effects on Fertility and Female Employment', in Moss, P. and Deven, F. (eds), *Parental Leave in Europe: Progress or Pitfall?*, The Hague/Brussels: NIDI/CBGS.

Ronsen, M. and Sundstrom, M. (1999), *Public Policies and the Employment Dynamics among New Mothers: A Comparison of Finland, Norway and Sweden*, Oslo: Statistics Norway, Discussion Paper No 263.

Rostgaard, T. and Fridberg, T. (1998), *Caring for Children and Older People – A Comparison of European Policies and Practices*, Copenhagen: The Danish National Institute of Social Research.

Ruddle, H., Donoghue, F. and Mulvihill, R. (1997), *The Years Ahead: A Review of the Implementation of its Recommendations*, Dublin: National Council on Ageing and Older People.

Ruhm, C.J. (1998), 'The Economic Consequences of Parental Leave Mandates: Lessons from Europe', *Quarterly Journal of Economics*, vol 113, no 1, pp. 285-317.

Ruxton, S. (1996), *Children in Europe*, London: NCH Action for Children.

Ruxton, S. (2001), 'Towards a 'Children's Policy' for the European Union?', in Foley, P., Roche, J. and Tucker, S. (eds), *Children in Society Contemporary Theory, Policy and Practice*, Basingstoke: Palgrave.

Schippers, J.J., Siegers, J.J. and de Jong-Gierveld, J. (eds) (1998), *Child Care and Female Labour Supply in the Netherlands*, Amsterdam: Thesis.

Second Commission on the Status of Women (1993), *Report,* Dublin: Stationery office.

Sgritta, G.B. (1990), 'Wege der Familienanalyse: Ein Überblick Über das letzte Jahrzehnt' in Lüscher, K., Schultheis, F. and Wehrspaun, M. (eds), *Die 'postmoderne' Familie: Familiale Strategien und Familienpolitik in einer Übergangszeit*, Konstanz: Universitätsverlag Konstanz.

Sharing in Progress National Anti-Poverty Strategy (1997), Dublin: Stationery Office.

Silva, E.B. and Smart, C. (eds) (1999), *The New Family?*, London: Sage.

Smart, C. (1997), 'Wishful Thinking and Harmful Tinkering? Sociological Reflections on Family Policy', *Journal of Social Policy*, vol 26, no 3, pp. 301-321.

Social Inclusion Strategy: Annual Report of the Interdepartmental Policy Committee (1999), Dublin: Stationery Office.

Sorensen, A. (1999), 'Family Decline, Poverty and Social Exclusion: The Mediating Effects of Family Policy', *Comparative Social Research*, vol 18, pp. 57-78.

Stainton Rogers, W. (2001), 'Constructing Childhood, Constructing Child Concern', in Foley, P., Roche, J. and Tucker, S. (eds), *Children in Society Contemporary Theory, Policy and Practice*, Basingstoke: Palgrave.

Szebehely, M. (1999), 'Concepts and Trends in Home Care for Frail Elderly People in France and in Sweden', in Palier, B. and Bouget, D. (eds), *Comparing Social Welfare Systems in Nordic Europe and France*, Paris: MIRE, vol 4.

Thélot, C. and Villac, M. (1998), *Politique Familiale: Bilan et Perspectives*, Paris: La Documentation Française.

Therborn, G. (1993), 'The Rights of Children since the Constitution of Modern Childhood: A Comparative Study of Western Nations', in Moreno, L. (ed), *Social Exchange and Welfare Development*, Madrid: Consejo Superior de Investigaciones Cientificas.

Thierry, M. and Palach, J. (1999), *Une Societé pour Tous les Ages*, Rapport du Comité de Pilotage de l'Année Internationale des Personnes Agées (http://www.social.gouv.fr).

Threlfall, M. (2000), 'Taking Stock and Looking Ahead' in Hantrais, L. (ed), *Gendered Policies in Europe: Reconciling Employment and Family Life*, Basingstoke: Macmillan.

Wennemo, I. (1994), *Sharing the Costs of Children Studies on the Development of Family Support in the OECD Countries*, Stockholm: Swedish Institute for Social Research.

Whyness, M.G. (2000), *Contesting Childhood*, London: Falmer Press.

Zimmerman, S. (1992), *Family Policies and Family Well-being*, Newbury Park: Sage.